MARKETPLACE ENDORSEMENTS

"Jack Serra has written a valuable book for those called to minister in the marketplace. He argues convincingly that the path to fruitfulness in both career and ministry leads first through a recommitment to a strong and godly marriage. His experience and insights shine a spotlight on this important prerequisite for seeing a great move of God in our communities."
—JANE RUMPH, AUTHOR, FREELANCE WRITER AND EDITOR, CALIFORNIA

I've heard wisdom defined as "knowledge plus experience." Jack has taken his 40 years of experience as both a businessman and husband and blended it with biblical principles to craft a work filled with practical wisdom. I would urge all "Marketplace Ministers" to use the wisdom of this book to dramatically increase their effectiveness regarding their God-given call. I would urge all husbands to firmly grasp these principles. I guarantee, from first-hand experience, this book will change your life (and your wife's)!
—HAL RICH, FORMER COO OF INSTINET CORP.; BOARD MEMBER DBS COMMUNICATIONS, BARRINGTON, ILLINOIS

Jack Serra's book, Marketplace, Marriage and Revival, *challenges the reader to understand the importance of marriage and its effect in spiritual growth in the marketplace. He clearly makes the case that unconditional love and unity in marriage contributes to the husband's spiritual prowess in the marketplace. Kudos, Jack.*
—REGINALD WILLIAMS, PASTOR AND COMMUNITY SERVICES DIRECTOR, VOLUSIA COUNTY, FLORIDA

Jack's book captures the paradox in Jesus' words, "For whoever wishes to save his life will lose it, but whoever loses his life for My sake and the gospel's will save it." Men, if you want to save your career and ministry, lose it and promote your wife's. If Jesus preached and lived out this message for His bride, the Church, how much more are His disciples to follow in His steps? Thank you, Jack, for pointing out the way (His way) to fruitfulness and fulfillment in career and ministry.

—RICK NEWTON, BUSINESS AND TECHNOLOGY
CONSULTANT, CLAYSVILLE, PENNSYLVANIA

Jack Serra speaks on the core issues for seeing revival come to our communities. He carries a message for a vital ingredient in presenting the truths of the gospel to our communities. The relationship of husband and wife is God's picture to the world of His relationship to the church. This book is a must-read for everyone in our generation.

—LAMAR & NANCY ESBENSHADE, ESBENSHADE'S
GREENHOUSES INC., EPHRATA, PENNSYLVANIA

God is using Jack Serra in a tremendous way to show us how our calling in the marketplace is uniquely connected to our wives (spouses) and families. The old paradigms and divisions between the secular, spiritual, personal, and professional identities are simply fading away. This is unity! As I have begun to pursue and bless my wife's identity, even sacrifice myself for the sake of knowing her, God is releasing both of us into our calling. And He is coming to work with me, not just as a program, but in prayer and presence.

—JIM KING, BUSINESS MANAGER, TAMPA, FLORIDA

One of the most significant by-products of the events of September 11 {2001}, is that Americans are getting their priorities back in order. I believe this book is a timely message for where we find

ourselves today. Jack Serra does a tremendous job bringing into focus the true priorities that we as ministering businessmen need to embrace in order to have effective ministries in these critical times.
—DEAN STEIN, COMMERCIAL LOAN BROKER
AND CONSULTANT, MARKETPLACE MINISTER, MOORESVILLE,
NORTH CAROLINA

As a Christian businessman, I know the importance of my call to reaching people for Christ and I am involved in "Sharing Christ Ministries" to do just that. Jack's book adds the new components of prayer evangelism and marriage that will give a greater assurance of our success in ministering in the marketplace and reaching the lost.
—DAVE NEUBAUER, BUSINESSMAN,
ORMOND BEACH, FLORIDA

PASTORS' ENDORSEMENTS

More and more people are responding to God's call to the marketplace. But Jack Serra is hearing an important sound that many have missed: "Your marriage will make the difference." Here is his book about marriage, business and revival; and Jack shows you how they all fit together. This book will be a valuable tool as we move into the exciting kingdom days ahead!
—RICH MARSHALL, PRESIDENT OF ROI EQUIPPING AND
AUTHOR OF GOD@WORK, SUNNYVALE, CALIFORNIA

"I don't just recommend this book because Jack has many challenging insights into the interface between marriage and the marketplace. I do so because he is pioneering into the relationship between the gospel and the world which is what more and more

of us must do, and he is courageously leading the way. You might not share his views on every issue. I don't, but I welcome his conclusions as a catalyst and challenge to my thinking and living. I am passionately convinced that the government of God has to penetrate every area of life. This book will help you explore how!"

—ROGER MITCHELL, PASSION, LONDON UK.

We can get as excited as we want about marketplace ministers, but they will never bear abundant fruit without godly character. Jack Serra agrees, and he pulls no punches in this stimulating book. He skillfully shows how what you are affects what you do. A Great Book!

—C. PETER WAGNER

Jack Serra is a dreamer of dreams and a seer of visions, a thoroughly practical man with his head in heaven. His story is funny at times, tender always and a faithful witness to the goodness of God. He has an important word for the whole church, not just those in the marketplace. Read and you'll pray as you read.

—BEN PATTERSON, DEAN OF CAMPUS MINISTRY, WESTMONT COLLEGE, SANTA BARBARA, CALIFORNIA

I am convinced that the devil hates balanced Christians. He loves Christians stressing one truth at the expense of another. He will hate this book! It is a must read for all who want to be part of the great reversal in our society when it comes to marriage breakdown. Serra's honest self-examination and biblical insight make this book special. It will challenge, exhort and encourage you to see the vital link between marriage, the marketplace and revival. Is this a key we have been missing?

—RICHARD TREACY, ANGLICAN PRIEST, IRELAND.

Jack Serra has put his finger on the Achilles heel of the American church. I recommend that every Christian businessman in America read this book. It will not only change your life and marriage, but it will change your perspective on how you see your profession. The message of this book must be heeded if the Church is to become relevant once again in the marketplace.

—FRANK WRAY, PASTOR OF BETHLEHEM COMMUNITY
CHURCH, BETHLEHEM, NEW YORK

I am encouraged by Marketplace, Marriage and Revival: The Spiritual Connection. *Jack Serra is not just a man with a vision, but one who is also committed to doing the work. This book contains more than just vision for revival; it is also very practical. It takes us and the gospel outside the walls of the church into our homes, businesses and community.*

—BYRON WICKER, SENIOR PASTOR, CALVARY COMMUNITY
CHURCH, MOORESVILLE, NORTH CAROLINA

Jack Serra has done an excellent job of laying out in easy-to-understand language how to tie together work, marriage and spiritual life. Every person involved in the marketplace needs to read this book.

—MITCH SMITH, PASTOR, MOTIVATIONAL SPEAKER,
EVANGELIST, STATE COLLEGE, PENNSYLVANIA

As numbers of voices are being raised, exposing the saints to their valuable ministry calling to the "marketplace," Jack Serra brings a balanced foundational focus back to cultivating a vital, fruitful marriage relationship first and foremost for successful ministry. With the newfound enthusiasm for marketplace ministry, we all need to hear this call.

—E. RALPH AND PATTI B. WALDEN, PASTORS, THRESHING
FLOOR MINISTRY AND BUSINESS OWNERS, BLYTHEWOOD,
SOUTH CAROLINA

Our Christian witness is greatly hampered if our marriage and family relationship are not a priority. Jack Serra writes from personal experience about how building one's marriage and family according to God's guidelines is essential spiritually and emotionally in our Christian influence at work, and in our relationship with God. This message is urgently needed by men today!

— DR. LARRY SELIG, PASTOR, PRESBYTERIAN CHURCH (USA), PITTSBURGH, PENNSYLVANIA

Since the first day I met jack Serra I have been impressed with the way God speaks so powerfully to others through his spoken words. Even greater than his anointed words is the way he has expressed his love for Christ in his daily walk as a Christian businessman and, more recently, a gospel minister. The strongest statement of our Lord's impact upon his life, however, is this personal account of the glorious spiritual transformation of his marriage and family life. I believe anyone who reads Jack's story will be inspired to ask Jesus Christ to shower their household with this same blessing and will, therefore, become better equipped in His service.

— REV. JIM SNYDER, DIRECTOR OF THE COMMUNITY MINISTRY INSTRUCTION NETWORK, PITTSBURGH, PENNSYLVANIA

We live in an age of uncertainty and more than ever we need godly people serving in the marketplace. Jack Serra's book is a valuable tool for opening our eyes to the legitimacy of ministry in the marketplace. Old paradigms that have limited our success in the marketplace are swept away and attention is focused on the power that comes to us when our marriages are biblically sound. The principles he presents are invaluable for those who want to reach whole cities for Christ.

— BOBBY SMITH, PASTOR, SOUTH DAYTONA CHRISTIAN CHURCH, DAYTONA BEACH, FLORIDA

This book is timely and needed. There is a lot of pressure on pastors and leaders in our day. Jack's book brings a word of hope that is based out of his experience and interaction with many hundreds of pastors and leaders. He is a man of integrity and committed to the things that he writes about. We have labored together and seen God come through with the principles that he writes about.

— ROY RHOADES, PASTOR AND SCHOOL TEACHER, HILTON HEAD, SOUTH CAROLINA

"Imagine, God wanting to answer your prayers, but won't because of a breech between you and your wife!" How about your business, ministry and family potential being limited due to unresolved conflicts within your family? Jack Serra's book covers a vast area of cross-over issues that a novice or expert in life, ministry and the Christian journey should have. This book is a must for all leaders from the corporate office to church office. This book is a must for the country church pastor and the city reacher visionary.

—MICHAEL A. MODICA, PASTOR & SHINE FLORIDA FACILITATOR

ACKNOWLEDGEMENTS

This book could never have been published without the help of a whole bunch of people. If we look at our lives we soon recognize that there is little if anything we can attribute to us alone. God always puts people in your path that become tremendous blessings and their presence helps mold you a bit more. I want to acknowledge,

- my son Jack, who was instrumental in my taking a critical promotion that led us to move to New Jersey in 1979 and three years later starting my first company. His selflessness freed me to move on and meet my destiny.

- Ed Silvoso, who has been my mentor for nine years and has transformed my thinking in life. He is my paradigm shifter and dear friend.

- Tom Tewell, my pastor and mentor for two years who helped me form my preaching and teaching skills.

- Ben Patterson, my pastor and mentor for four crucial years from 1989-1993 by leading me into the things of God and understanding my revival, marriage and how to enjoy being a Christian. Ben is a real man.

- Rich Krznaric, my pastor and mentor from 1993-1999. Rich taught me patience and wisdom. His preaching was a breath of fresh air that filled my heart.

- Donn Chapman, my present pastor who allowed me to use his message on obedience for this book. His council has been valuable.

- Rock Dillaman, past president of the Christian Missionary Alliance church who unwittingly added many great thoughts for my book through his preaching.

-Hal Rich and Don Spencer, two of the three City Slickers (I was the third) who were a sounding board and friends at every turn since 1990. We have had many long talks about our lives as men of Christ. They were very profitable.

- Roger Wilkin, who poured his life into me shortly after we moved to New Jersey and continues to do so.

- Murray and Donna Fisher who agreed to publish this book. They are more than publishers. They are lovers of Christ and our new friends. This book wouldn't exist without Murray's guidance and expertise.

FOREWORD BY ED SILVOSO

Marketplace
Marriage
& Revival

The Spiritual Connection

Jack Serra

First printing: April 2002
Second printing: August 2003

Printed in the United States of America

Published by Longwood Communications
3037 Clubview Drive, Orlando, FL 32822
407-737-6006

Unless otherwise noted, all Scripture quotations are from
the Holy Bible, New International Version. Copyright ©
1973, 1978, 1984 by International Bible Society. Used by
permission.

Materials quoted from *The God Chasers* by Tommy
Tenney, copyright © 1998, used by permission of
Destiny Image Publishers, P.O. Box 310, Shippensburg,
PA 17257

Materials quoted from *The Fire of His Holiness* by Sergio
Scataglini, copyright © 1999, Regal Books, division of
Gospel Light, Ventura, CA.

A TRIBUTE TO ALICE JANE, MY WIFE

One evening Alice Jane and I were talking about our relationship and just how we saw each other. Throughout the conversation, Alice Jane kept lifting me up, without giving herself any recognition at all. I tried to give her recognition, but she wouldn't receive it. Then it hit me! The book that you are about to read is a tribute to Alice Jane, my wife. It's a tribute to Alice Jane because it's all about how God used her wisdom, love, anointed opinions and strength to make a good marriage a godly one. It's a tribute to Alice Jane because she is the one whom God used to correct my flaws, as well as my lack of understanding of my role as a godly husband. It is a tribute to her because thousands of men and women will now know what we know about marriage, simply because she stayed the course and kept both of us straight. It's a tribute to her because our children really know who she is in Christ.

Nothing you do could be more important than to see your children reflect upon your life as a

Christian parent and tell you what you've meant to them. Alice Jane has always been a great wife, mother and grandmother, but I have only recently recognized her great gifts of unconditional love, anointed opinions, wisdom and steadfastness. One of the sections in this book is titled, "Do You See What I See?" God once asked me if I saw what He saw in my wife. I didn't, but He showed me and it transformed my life and our marriage. What I considered the problem was in reality the solution.

Alice Jane was already submitting to me, but I wasn't leading in a godly manner. Thank you, Alice Jane Ruckle, for being my wife. You are a true blessing, and I finally see what God sees in you. Thank you, God, for Your gift of my wife. I pray that You see her better off now than when You gave her to me. I pray, Alice Jane, that your life will continue to have a tremendous spiritual impact on our family and beyond for a thousand generations.

LOVE ALWAYS,

JACK

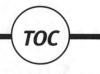

FOREWORD

ED SILVOSO

In the Book of Revelation the Lord Jesus instructed John to send letters to seven churches, each with a specific message from the Lord Himself. Each one ended with the admonition that he who has an ear should hear what the Spirit is saying to the churches. This is illustrative of the fact that from time to time the Lord may choose to highlight certain truths, and He wants us to be attentive to His voice, the Holy Spirit. Consequently, those who have made themselves available to the Lord to listen to His voice, need to be on the alert so that the message won't be lost.

Jack Serra is one of those spiritual listeners. He wrote, *Marketplace, Marriage and Revival: The Spiritual Connection* out of obedience to the Lord. He felt the Lord depositing revelatory thoughts, first in his mind and then on his heart about Christianity in the marketplace. Definitely, a new paradigm affecting the church. The heart of the message entrusted to Jack is that the marketplace is the heart of the city, and that taking the kingdom of God to the marketplace is the key to see our cities transformed. But for this to happen we need to see our marriage strengthened and not weakened by our business career. Jack's message is timely, clear and much needed.

Jack Serra, a businessman by training and a minister by calling, addresses in this book one of the most important issues affecting the marketplace today: marriage and business. Time and again we see that when a person reaches the pinnacle of success in business, they lose their marriage along the way. What is the use of commanding the attention of peers and employees while losing the respect and the affection of the person to whom he or she has pledged spirit, soul and body?

Jack Serra, writes from the vantage point of a practitioner. He is not a theoretician but one who has been there and has chosen to stay there! God has blessed Jack with a wonderful wife, A.J., and a very successful career in business in the pharmaceutical industry. While in the business world, Jack and A.J. faithfully used their influence and material resources to expand the kingdom of God while modeling godliness at home and in marriage. Later on, they gave up their business to help pastors reach their cities for Christ through prayer evangelism. While doing this, Jack came to the realization that unless Christians in the marketplace are equipped and deployed, cities will not be reached. As he looked further into it, he discovered that the key lies with strengthening the marriages of those called to serve in the marketplace. "A man's ministry in the marketplace will only advance to the extent his marriage permits," Jack likes to say.

Marketplace, Marriage and Revival is a how-to book on how to strengthen your marriage in order to strengthen your career. Jack writes with humor, plenty of illustrations and straight to the point exhortations. This book is a definite must read for every Christian in the marketplace. I have been greatly blessed by *Marketplace, Marriage and Revival,* and I know you will too.

ED SILVOSO
AUTHOR, *That None Should Perish, Prayer Evangelism, Women-God's Secret Weapon,* AND *Anointed For Business*

1

The Enemy Attacked While We Were Sleeping

9-11: The Old War Steps Up

The World Trade Center attack was a direct assault on the marketplace. Have you ever wondered why the evildoers who despise Christianity didn't attack some significant buildings used for Christian purposes instead of the World Trade Center and the Pentagon? Recognizing that the enemy, Satan, is behind all of this, we must look at his thoughts and plans instead of those we attribute to Osama bin Laden. The battle is always in the heavenlies, between the forces of evil and the angels. Just as the Holy Spirit is in control of our lives if we are Christians, Satan has direct control of Osama bin Laden's life.

IT'S ABOUT SATAN, NOT OSAMA BIN LADEN

My theory is that the enemy saw the beginnings of a massive buildup of a new army made up of Christians who work in government, education and business. This must have caused great concern for him, as he remembered two occasions since his fall from heaven when he lost thousands of his most prized possessions: souls. The first was when the Holy Spirit came upon the 120 followers of Christ in the upper room and they ended up in the marketplace. The Holy Spirit chased them out of the Upper Room so that they could meet the lost. On that day, three thousand were saved. Where? In the marketplace.

The second occasion occurred in 1857, when Jeremiah Lamphier began a prayer meeting that eventually filled the churches of New York City to overflowing. A reporter was sent by his newspaper to count the number of men praying in the churches and had to stop at fourteen thousand to make his deadline. It wasn't long before this prayer meeting spread to Washington, D.C., where nine thousand men were found praying—and to Philadelphia and Pittsburgh where six thousand were counted. Soon the revival moved across the northern United States. One million people were saved in the United States. And where and how did the revival begin? In the marketplace, through a businessman.

1857 AND 2001: REVIVAL IS AT HAND

The prayer meetings that began in New York in 1857 started in the shadow of what would become the World Trade Center and Wall Street. The enemy had seen revival flourish once in New York, and he doesn't want to see it happen again. So he used the terrorists to hit the World Trade Center, the epicenter of our nation's financial marketplace. He tried to scare us with this attack, but instead he galvanized the entire country and started them praying. The 1857 revival began with prayer, and this coming revival could be strengthened by the prayers that rise from the ashes of the World Trade Center.

No one can remember the last time prayer was so prevalent in our society. It's everywhere. Our nation's lawmakers sang "God Bless America" on the Capitol steps. Churches overflowed on September 16, 2001. People are praying in airports, hotel lobbies, on the streets, in schools, in government buildings, on the radio, and even on CNN, as when T.D. Jakes was asked to pray for our country during an interview. The marketplace is being filled with prayer. Who would have ever thought it possible? Throughout our country, the spiritual climate has changed dramatically.

WE NEED TO PREPARE—NOW!

The major problem we face as a nation and as the church is that we were not prepared for this atrocity. We were living in a dream world, where nothing truly bad could happen in our country. We had just experienced a decade of tremendous prosperity, and we were living a life so exceptional that we had become complacent. We were fully convinced that the economic growth—the "good life"—would continue forever, or at least for a very long time.

We were asleep, now we are awake. An earthshaking jolt has knocked us out of bed and onto our knees, and we now know that we are at war—both physically and spiritually. There's something that war does to us. It gets us angry and causes us to reflect on life and become more spiritual.

Knowing we are at war and have a fierce enemy unites our hearts and minds, and places a resolve deep within our nation's soul. We know and understand that the enemy is relentless, but we must also know that he cannot win the war. There is no truce in this war. Perseverance is required. God's ways are not our ways. Love, holiness, prayer and trust are key to winning the battles we will face. Unity is the key to any successful army.

As Christians, we always win, but it is more difficult from a defensive posture and it takes longer. We need to assume an offensive posture so we can see the spiritual climate change in our cities and country. So, how do we get into an offensive position as the body of Christ? A major portion of God's army is found in the marketplace. They are salespeople, secretaries, CEO's, janitors, plumbers, teachers, entertainers, authors, firefighters, police, mayors, county commissioners, and countless others who work in education, government, or business.

THE PURPOSE OF THIS BOOK

This book has been written so that Christian men can better understand their calling in the workplace and the absolute requirement of a strong and vital marriage, especially if we hope to see a great move of God in our lifetime. Another purpose of this book is to help you understand that God expects you to treat your wife in a certain manner—and if you don't, your prayers for the marketplace could be hindered (1 Pet. 3:7).

There are many wonderful books and seminars on revival, marketplace ministry and marriage, but we need to see these as inextricably linked. Otherwise, we will not experience the fullness of what God is planning. Ed Silvoso does a wonderful job, in his new book *Anointed for Business*, demonstrating how marketplace leaders played a key role in the emergence, establishment and expansion of the early church. The same should be true today. Ed also tells us that God has anointed people to minister in the marketplace, that work can be a joy and that the marketplace is the heart of the city. You really need to pick up a copy of *Anointed for Business* and be released into your calling.

I speak from the perspective of a businessman who has been married for 41 years and who in the past seven has only begun to understand the significance of having a godly marriage. I also write as one who has worked in the marketplace for 34 years. I spent 21 years working for a major pharmaceutical company and thirteen years as the owner of three businesses. In 1988, I received the coveted "Entrepreneur of the year award" from Ernst & Young for my company, Arista. I've been an employee and an employer. I have seen both sides of the coin.

WHEN GOD CALLS, YOU SHOULD ANSWER

Since 1993 when God called us back to Pittsburgh, we've been on a new path that was totally unexpected. Within six weeks, we lost two of our three companies and one-third of our wealth. Shortly after these losses we met Ed Silvoso, founder of Harvest Evangelism. He explained to us that we had been called by God to reach cities for Christ. Originally, we thought that meant we were called to minister from the marketplace, but we soon learned that we would have no place in the marketplace from which to minister. In 1996, we lost our third company, and in 1997, we lost our home and all we had.

God had His plan, and we were falling into it rather dramatically. Throughout this time, we began to serve with Ed and found ourselves ministering among pastors in numerous communities. By 1996, A.J. and I believed we were being called out of the marketplace and into ministry with Harvest Evangelism. This meant we had to change our lives in ways we could never have imagined a few years earlier. We would soon have to begin raising our own support in order to minister with Harvest. As I write this book, I am Harvest Evangelism's vice president of ministries for the eastern United States. I believe this day was planned by God, as long ago as the day when I received Jesus as my Lord and Savior in October 1977. Then, I only knew that I was embarking on a path where God was leading, and I prayed that He would use my life in some unique way. But the fact of the matter is, God has a unique path for each of us.

MEETING THE TWO MOST IMPORTANT PEOPLE IN MY LIFE

The excitement of meeting Jesus was like none other I'd felt in my life—that is, apart from the evening I first saw Alice Jane. It was 1958, and I was 17 and a senior in high school. My friend Mike and I had just walked into the Italian Club in my hometown of Pitcairn, P.A. My hometown was a place where the people loved to dance. Often a number of high school girls from the neighboring town of Trafford came to our dances, and that evening two girls from Trafford showed up. The moment I saw Alice Jane (A.J.) across the crowded dance floor, I said to Mike, "See that girl over there? I'm going to marry her."

"The one on the left?" Mike asked.

"No, the one on the right," I said. I didn't know her name and had certainly never seen her before, yet somehow deep in my soul, I knew what I said was true. We were married on October 27, 1962.

It was that same feeling when I met Jesus for the first time. I knew I had to follow Him wherever He would take me, but I hadn't a clue what that meant. Then again, I hadn't really known what it meant to be married, either. I just knew it would be great. I knew that night in April of 1958 that I had the right woman in my life—and now it was October, 1977, and I had the right Lord in my life. My life changed dramatically that day in April, and it changed in an even greater way that October day some nineteen years later. Prior to that time, something had been missing from my life, and A.J. knew just what it was.

REMEMBER TO PUT THE BIG ROCKS IN FIRST

Once an expert in time management was speaking to a group of business students, and to drive a point home, he used an illustration the students would never forget.

Standing before the group of high-powered over-achievers, he said, "Okay, time for a quiz." He pulled out a one-gallon widemouthed mason jar and placed it on the table in front of him. Then he produced about a dozen rocks the size of your fist, and carefully put them, one by one, into the jar. When the jar was filled to the top and no more rocks would fit inside, he asked, "Is the jar full?"

Everyone in the class said, "Yes."

Then he said, "Really?" He reached under the table and pulled out a bucket of gravel. He dumped some gravel in and shook the jar, causing the pieces of gravel to work themselves into the spaces between the big rocks. Then he asked the class once more, "Is the jar full?"

By this time the students were on to him. "Probably not," someone answered.

"Good," he replied. Now, he reached under the table and brought out a bucket of sand. As he poured the sand into the jar, it filled all the spaces between the rocks and the gravel. Once again the man asked the question, "Is the jar full?"

"No!" the class shouted.

Then the man grabbed a pitcher of water and began to pour it into the jar, until it was filled to the brim.

Then the time-management expert asked the class, "What is the point of this illustration?"

One eager beaver raised his hand and said, "The point is, no matter how full your schedule is, if you really try hard you can always fit some more things in it."

"No!" the speaker replied, "that's not the point! The truth this illustration teaches is this: If you don't put the big rocks in first, you'll never get them in at all. What are the big rocks in your life? Your spouse? Your children? Your loved ones? Your work? Your friendships? Your education? Your dreams? A worthy cause? Your health? Doing the things you love to do? God? Remember to put these big rocks in first, or you'll never get them in at all. If you concern yourself with the little stuff (like the gravel and the sand) you'll fill your life with little things and never have the quality time you need to spend on the big, important stuff. Remember, it's *you* who decides what the big rocks are."

So, what are your big rocks in life? They should be God, your wife, your children and work.

GOD'S LOVE VERSUS OUR LOVE

Those of us who are married or who plan to get married need to know that the spouse we choose will be critical to every aspect of the rest of our lives. Marriage is a very important "big rock." I can state with all honesty that I am writing this book because of my wife and her role in my life. But it is even more important to know that we must fall in love with the living God. There is a major difference between these two relationships. No matter how much I loved Alice Jane, she had to say "yes" and love me back. My love for her was not sufficient for us to be married. She had to accept my love and return her love. My love and hers were conditional.

With God it's totally different. He loves us first, but He also loves us unconditionally. He demonstrated that *agape* love by sending His Son to die for us. We, in turn, must receive that love, repent of our sins, and ask Him to come into our lives. While Alice Jane needed to respond favorably to my love, we need to respond favorably to God's love. The difference is,

God's love is unconditional. It doesn't depend on my response. My love depended on A.J.'s response. It was conditional.

I once heard that a prostitute, when asked why she had eight children, responded by saying, "I'm just trying to give birth to unconditional love." How sad is that? Unable to find the love she craved in life, she thought it would come through a child. Actually, it did—nearly two thousand years ago. God gave birth to unconditional love a long time ago, and all we must do is accept it and offer it to others.

I have since learned that these two relationships—a relationship with Jesus Christ and with a spouse—are the most critical and foundational to a walk with God, as well as to how we will live out our lives in the marketplace for God. So often we build a relationship with God at the expense of our relationship with our wives. You need to know, as I eventually found out, that it's impossible to build a complete relationship with God without building a strong and vital relationship with your wife. Likewise, you can't build a complete relationship with your wife if you haven't built a strong and vital relationship with God. The two go hand in hand and are not mutually exclusive. In fact, if you're married, they are fully dependent upon one another.

REACHING THE MARKETPLACE FOR CHRIST IS DEPENDENT ON YOUR MARRIAGE

"Your city will be won from your bedroom." This statement came as a casual comment from Dave Thompson, executive vice president for Harvest, about three years ago. I believed it to be true then, and I believe it's true today. One of the most important keys to reaching your city through the marketplace is your marriage. You can't expect to fulfill Paul's instructions in Philippians 2:1-5 corporately if you aren't fulfilling them in the most basic of relationships, marriage. Paul exhorts us to be like-minded, having the same love and being one in spirit and purpose ... to do nothing out of selfish ambition or vain conceit, but in humility, to consider others better than ourselves. We're also commanded to look to the interests of others. These verses from Philippians apply directly to our marriages, and if we are double-minded about the necessity of a sound marriage, we cannot fully reach the marketplace for Christ, let alone a city.

It's clear to me that we must do what Paul says—at home before we do it with others. After all, who are the "others" to whom Paul is referring? No one in particular is implied in these verses; therefore, it must mean everyone. Your friends and your neighbors. Your boss and your subordinates. Those who despise you. Everyone. But first, it means your wife. And what does Paul say we're to do? Imitate Christ's humility and let our attitude be the same as that of Christ Jesus.

This book will help you examine and strengthen your relationship with your wife, so that you can serve God right where He has called you to minister—in the marketplace. It's about really knowing that a strong and holy marriage is a prerequisite for fulfilling one's God-given destiny in the marketplace, and thereby, creating a foundation for revival and a great move of God in our day. It's about achieving one's full potential as God's representative in the marketplace and as an agent for revival.

A New Key Component for Revival

I believe God is giving us a vision for the marketplace and for those who work within it. The vision is that we live in a time when God is prepared to release marketplace people to reach the marketplace for Christ. Now is the time to step up to the plate and have marketplace people come together and pray for their companies, their employers, their employees and even the competition. The direction is clearly for each Christian in the marketplace to see his job as his ministry.

However, there is another key aspect if you're married. You see, as I began this book, God said something very clearly to me: "A businessman's ministry will only advance to the extent that his marriage permits." That means that your success as a businessman and as a minister within the marketplace depends on the wholeness of your marriage. This truth applies in the realms of education and government as well.

Since writing this book, I have read dozens of books on marriage, and they run the gamut, covering almost every aspect of married life. However, to my knowledge, none of these books has connected the importance of a godly, holy marriage with revival, awakening and the marketplace.

God wants believers in the marketplace to understand our true and full calling. A calling is almost always more than we can understand at the moment we receive it. We are certainly called to see our jobs as ministries, but we must also see that a person's marriage plays a critical role in developing his ministry in the marketplace. You see, while the underpinnings for revival are prayer and unity—and while pastors and intercessors are instrumental in calling forth revival—it is equally important that you and I understand what role we play as people working in the marketplace and as husbands and wives.

You need to know that you have left your father and mother to be united to your wife, and that the two of you have become one flesh. Paul tells us, "This is a profound mystery" (Eph. 5:32). One of the reasons this remains a profound mystery is that we have chosen not to discuss this issue. Most of us have decided we can't figure it out, or that if we do figure it out, it will only cause major problems in your marriage. So we don't talk about it. Unfortunately, burying the issue never solves the problem. Instead, we miss knowing all God has purposed for us, and therefore we live less than full lives in Christ. This has resulted in a higher divorce rate among Christians than in other groups.

By ignoring our calling in marriage, we miss the greatest opportunity to see God move in our lives, across the marketplace, and throughout our cities, states, and nation in full revival. That's right: how we respond to God's calling in our marriages will be a determining factor in leading the body of Christ to experience revival and reach the lost.

Almost sounds impossible, doesn't it? It's not! Nothing God calls us to is impossible for Him. It will take prayer, unconditional love, intention, perseverance, leadership, submission and much more. However, it's worth it. Lives, both saved and lost, depend upon our desire to be successful in our marriages and to reach the marketplace for Christ.

I sometimes imagine God meeting me in heaven. In my mind's eye, He approaches me, and I immediately begin to think about my sins, my work life, my prayer life, how much I read His Word, my ministry, and so on. As I wait for Him to speak, I wonder if I'll get a "Well done, good and faithful servant!" What will He say? Will He ask about my quiet time? The tension builds with each passing moment. My heart is pounding. My palms are sweating, and time seems to be standing still. All of a sudden, God is standing right in front of me. It's Him! As I stare into His face, my mind races faster and faster. *What will God say?* Then He speaks.

"So, Jack, how's Alice Jane?"

What did He say? How's Alice Jane?

"Yes, how's Alice Jane?"

What would your answer be? Join me in determining to make the second most important relationship in your life—your relationship with your wife—all that God would have it be, so that you can see God move deeper in your life and marriage as well as across your neighborhood, marketplace, and city to reach the lost.

We will not see full and lasting revival in our cities without first seeing men who work in the marketplace taking their position in God's plan and ushering in the revival God intends to bring forth. Do you want to see a great move of God in your city? You are being called to usher it in, right where you work and live. So step forward in the marketplace and be anointed by God. But if you are married, don't do it without your wife.

2

"So, How's Your Wife?" In Love With Life and the World

Marriage, Success and Kids

I always wanted to be married, have kids, and have a very successful career. If you're reading this book, you've probably wanted the same things. As long as I can remember, I wanted to be a big success and make a lot of money. Apparently, my classmates expected this of me too, since they voted me "most likely to succeed" among my graduating class at Pitcairn High. To be honest, I really didn't care what I did so much as how much money and prestige I could attain. There was absolutely no pressure from my parents in this area. In fact, I had a very happy and pleasant childhood that was totally devoid of stress from outside sources. I alone applied all the stress necessary to make me a driven, "type A" person. I was so competitive at Little League baseball that they almost threw me off the team for arguing with the umpires. Sound familiar?

I'm convinced that most successful people are "type A" people. It doesn't really matter why you're driven to succeed, it's a problem regardless of the reason. Someone who is driven has already made up his mind that the thing that drives him is the most important thing he can do; everything else ranks a distant second. Typically, a driven person won't listen to anyone because he already has his mind made up. Sometimes he doesn't even know he is driven. It isn't always about money, titles, or prestigious positions either, though in my case these were the driving factors. It's really about being driven to be the best at what you do. You can be an extremely successful executive, doctor, lawyer, entrepreneur, dentist, or professor—and not be a "type A" personality. On the other hand, you can be a middle manager, secretary, dental assistant, nurses' aide, elementary school teacher, detective, housewife, plumber or electrician and be "type A."

WHERE DO YOU FIND THE TIME?

Remember, I wanted a happy marriage, kids and a successful career. The problem was there wasn't enough room in my life for all these desires, especially since I came from a small town and was the first to attend college in my family. My grandparents were immigrants from northern Italy, and both of my grandfathers worked in a coal mine. My father worked for Westinghouse Air Brake, prior to buying a confectionery in our hometown. He purchased the store in 1952, and it was strategically located across the street from the only walking bridge to the railroad yards. I was

12 at the time and insisted on working a shift daily. I first knew I was an entrepreneur when I decided to take the sno-cone machine outside the store during our town's annual firemen's parades each summer. No one was coming in to the store because of the parade, so I took the product to the people. It worked.

As I started high school, I realized that becoming a doctor would give me what I really wanted: prestige and lots of money. When I entered the University of Pittsburgh in 1958, it only took one semester and a "D" in chemistry to reveal that medicine wasn't for me. But that didn't stop me. What about dentistry? Two years later and a few more "D's" in the sciences removed any possibility of my becoming a dentist. *What do I do now? Just finish college,* I thought. And so I did.

OFF TO FIND SUCCESS WITH MY WIFE

In 1962, I married Alice Jane. Following our wedding, we drove virtually nonstop to Los Angeles with all of our earthly possessions in a 1959 Volkswagen. I thought L.A. would be the place where I could make it big and achieve the success I craved. My first job was as a bacteriologist in a testing lab for dairy products. That lasted six months. I quickly recognized I was going nowhere.

"I'M MISSING IT"

I left there to accept a job as a pharmaceutical salesman for J.B. Roerig & Co. Within months I was the number one salesman in the district, and within a year I was the number one salesman in the region. Now, this was more like it.

17

In 1963 we decided to request a transfer to Pittsburgh since we wanted to adopt children and needed to be in a stable environment. Both our families lived in Pittsburgh at the time. Between 1963 and 1977 I had numerous jobs. During those years I lost one of my jobs and joined CIBA Pharmaceutical. We had to leave Pittsburgh once again and live in Springfield, Illinois, and later in St. Louis, Missouri. In 15 years, I held six jobs with five companies in four cities—and I had not advanced at all. I was still a salesman and growing very bored with life.

We had three children during that time, and by 1977 Jack was 12, Jim was 10, and Kristin was four. I was no further ahead in my pursuit of prestige and money than when I had begun. At 37, I was becoming too old to be promoted and almost too old to change careers. I had dragged my family across the country and still hadn't found what I was looking for in life. I almost began to succumb to the thought that I would never achieve what I had been chasing.

The Most Important Moment in My Life

In October of 1977, my wife and I were having dinner at the Barn Dinner Theater in St. Louis. During the first intermission, I confessed to her that I hadn't been feeling fulfilled and couldn't understand why. After all, I had a wonderful wife, three great children, a nice home and a good job. But there was something missing. A.J.'s immediate response was, "Maybe it's because we don't have Christ in our lives."

Now, that was an amazing statement since neither one of us had ever heard that you needed Him as your personal Savior and we'd agreed never to talk about religion once we were married. I had promised to allow A.J. to raise the kids in the Lutheran church while I went golfing.

Equally amazing was my response: "I think you're right, but what do we do now?"

SALVATION AND SUCCESS COME THROUGH A BUSINESSMAN

A.J. and I were two unbelievers seeking Christ without a believer in sight. I told my wife I knew of a salesman for another pharmaceutical company who always had a Bible in the back seat of his car. His name was John Council. On Monday morning I went to Barnes Hospital to see if I could find him. The night before, John had prayed that God would make it easy for him to witness to someone. He had difficulty talking about Christ. As I entered the hospital, I saw John and rushed up to him and blurted out, "John, can you tell me anything about Jesus?" How's that for God answering his prayer? John appeared quite startled, but gathered himself and invited me for a cup of coffee. We spent two hours talking about Jesus.

As I write this on my computer, I realize now that my salvation was the product of prayer evangelism in the marketplace. John was a businessman. I came to Christ because a businessman prayed that God would make it easy for him to witness to someone. I was that someone and so was my wife. Just look at how it all unfolded. My wife was hearing the Word at a Lutheran church (that's how she knew to mention Jesus), while I was golfing. John was afraid to witness, but just at the right time he prayed for God to make it easy. In I walked the very next morning. Coincidence? I think not! My salvation is the product of a businessman who simply carried his Bible in his car and asked God to make witnessing easy. God works with us just where we are, whatever our level of obedience and courage.

JOHN GETS PROMOTED?
WHAT ABOUT ME, LORD?

In the fall of 1978, I ran into John Council at Barnes Hospital. He told me he'd just been promoted to a job in the home office of his company. I told him how happy I was for him and how much I'd always wanted the same position in my own firm. He told me to do what he had done: pray for the job. That was too much for me to comprehend. Until now, I'd been doing it my way. I certainly couldn't bother God for something so trivial as a promotion, could I? Well, I did. I prayed for God to give me a promotion. In a few weeks I received a call from the home office and a job offer in Chicago. But as I pursued the job offer, I became more and more convinced that it wasn't for me. It was a promotion I had been seeking for years, and now that I prayed for it, someone really wanted me. But nothing seemed to work out. The salary was not enough to justify the move. The houses in Chicago were more expensive too. I refused the offer.

I thought I had blown it completely. How could I have turned down my first promotion, at age 39? Was I crazy? No. I believe God was testing me, to see if I would jump at the first thing that came my way. I know now that if I had taken that job, I wouldn't be where I am today. What God knew that I didn't was that a man in the sales promotion department was praying for Him to send a Christian to fill a position that was perfect for me. I didn't know it at the time and only learned about his prayers some months after taking the job. Now, pay attention closely. Silvio Coccia, the man praying in the home office, was both a Christian and a businessman. All the odds were against my getting the job. But God wanted me there, and He caused the businessman, Silvio, and me to pray together— without either of us knowing that the other one was praying. If God wants you to get a promotion or a new business, He will make a way where there seems to be no way.

I believe that from this prayer forward, God had me on a path that He had prepared in advance for me that I might walk in it. (See Ephesians 2:10.) All of a sudden, I received four promotions in three years. All those years without a promotion were made up for in three short years. During the next few years, God prepared and equipped me to start my own company with a couple of men who owned another small business that served the pharmaceutical industry. So, in 1983 we started Arista Marketing Associates.

How Big Is Your God?

The point of the story of my praying for a promotion centers around something my friend, Sebastian, from Ghana once asked me. He asked if I would go to Ghana so that I could see how big Satan is. When I asked why I should go all the way to Ghana just to see how big Satan is, he replied, "Because, you will see how big God is."

I told my friend that I thought the God we both worshipped was the same big God, and he responded with another question: "Jack, what would you do in order to get to New York City on time for a 1 o'clock meeting?" We lived in New Jersey at the time, and I told him that I would leave at 11:00 to be sure I was there on time.

He said, "In Ghana when we want to make it to a meeting in Accra, we have to pray that the bus will come. If it does come, we must pray that it will arrive at our stop on time; then we must pray that it will not break down on the way to our meeting. "You see," he continued, "we have to pray for all the little things in our lives while you just take care of them on your own. You only pray for the things you can't do on your own—and that's not much in America. Our God is bigger than yours."

I stood in my kitchen with my mouth hanging open, realizing I had no response. He was right. As the body of Christ, we have eliminated God from the ordinary things of life just because we can take care of them ourselves. We're smart enough, aren't we? We can handle the small stuff.

Is a promotion part of the small stuff? Is where you go to school, live, or shop small stuff? Is who you marry part of the small stuff as well? God wants to be involved in all we do in life, and He wants to guide us through this life and into the next. The fact of the matter is that only He can! We need to pray about every aspect of life, don't we?

It's time we invited God back into the small things in our lives. If I hadn't prayed for that job, who knows where I would be now? Only God does. I've been talking about how we men typically go about our lives without knowing God. We live as the world lives, and that's normal for us when we don't know Christ as Lord and Savior. However, once we do come to a saving knowledge of Christ we can't stop there. It is imperative to know that our jobs and marriages are critical to God's next great move.

SUMMARY POINTS

- Your relationships with God and your wife are not mutually exclusive.
- As a "type A" personality, you don't have room for all you desire in life when your job becomes number one.
- My wife and I came to Christ through a praying businessman.
- God will always make a way for you to be His witness when you see your job as your ministry.
- It's fine to pray for your job and promotions, but recognize that God already has a path prepared in advance for you that you might walk in it. Consider His will for your life.

3

SUCCESS IS WHEN OPPORTUNITY MEETS PREPAREDNESS

The title of this chapter comes from a statement I heard or read about 30 years ago. From the world's perspective, it is a truism. You can't be successful if the opportunity comes and you aren't prepared. Neither can you be successful if you aren't given an opportunity to succeed, no matter how prepared you become. Aside from what we call luck, success is likely when these two things meet—opportunity and preparedness. Ultimately, success—however it is achieved—is a poor substitute for God and a failing source of true significance.

I'M SUCCESSFUL AND RICH

Remember when I told you how much I wanted to be rich and successful? Well, it happened. I was prepared, and the opportunity came. What I failed to realize fully at the time was that it was God who allowed me to be prepared; it was also He who provided the opportunity. In March of 1983, I started Arista with two men who were excellent at business but who were not believers. That was a mistake that would eventually prove disastrous. If I knew then what I know now, it might have been different. But I didn't, and it wasn't.

From 1983 to 1988, the company doubled in size each year and continued to grow until 1991. My income followed the same trend. I went from a salary of 60 thousand dollars in 1982 to two million a year in 1988. For the next four years, I earned two million a year. On top of it all, I was selected 1988 New Jersey "Entrepreneur of the Year" by Ernst & Young. This is a coveted award, and the competition is tremendous. As of the year 2000, there are only a few more than three thousand people in the world who have received this honor.

I had finally arrived at the goal I had chased since I was a young man in Pitcairn, working in my dad's store. If you're expecting me to say that I didn't find what I was looking for through success and money, you're wrong. You see, I already knew that Jesus was the most important person in my life, and nothing—money nor prestige—could change that.

Do You Feel Guilty About Your Success? Don't!

Believers today have an erroneous notion that the Bible says, "Money is the root of all evil." I can't tell you how many people thought that money would be bad for A.J. and me—our ruination. As a matter of fact, when we lost it all in 1997, many Christians came up to us and said things like, "I'm sure you're happier, now that you don't have money." *Wrong!* We were very disappointed to lose our money. Christian people who have never experienced wealth haven't a clue as to what it means. Can we get one biblical point straight? The Bible says that, "The *love of* money is a root of all kinds of evil" (1 Tim. 6:10, emphasis added)—not *money*, but the *love of* money. What would happen to ministries and churches if we didn't have money to support them? And note that the Bible doesn't say that money is *the root*, but *a root*—and it doesn't say that money is the root of *all* evil, but *all kinds* of evil. There are many other roots and many kinds of evil.

Money is like power or position. It can be used for good or for evil. Power, position and wealth are neutral. Alone, they can do nothing. If someone chooses to use his wealth and position only for himself or to destroy others it can be very bad. But, if that same person chooses to use these things to edify and support others, it can be very good. If we don't reject this poverty mentality embraced by much of the body of Christ, we will never advance the kingdom of God.

IT'S NOT ABOUT MONEY
(WELL, MAYBE JUST A LITTLE BIT)

I want to tell you something right up front. Don't feel guilty or uncomfortable about your wealth or success. If God has placed you in such a position, you should be filled with great joy and excitement. If He put you there, it's for an amazing purpose. One reason He places people in a higher income bracket is to have witnesses among the wealthy. Remember that Zacchaeus was very wealthy and a scoundrel as well; yet Jesus visited his home and Zacchaeus responded properly. If you are in a position of wealth or prestige, it's because God needs you there to serve Him in this coming revival.

I was watching a television interview with Bill Gates recently, and the interviewer asked about his house. When the journalist began making statements like, "I understand it cost $60 million and that you can listen to music under water in your pool," you could see Bill getting a bit sheepish. Then the interviewer asked, "Why are you so embarrassed having these things when you're worth $100 billion?"

I'll never forget his answer. Gates said, and I quote, "Well, you see, the more I consume on myself, the less I have to give away." Imagine that! I have read that Gates intends to give away all of his money, leaving only $10 million to each of his children. As Ed Silvoso would say, "Let the Holy Spirit speak to you now." There's a very good reason to have money, isn't there? To give it away as God directs.

But that's not what this book is about. Sure, money is always involved, and you can't get around that. But this book is about activating your God-given calling in the marketplace so that Christ can be lifted up and the lost can be found, right where you work. It's about your developing a relationship with your wife so that nothing will ever destroy it. It's about knowing that if your marriage is whole, your prayers won't be hindered in your business.

We are told to seek first His kingdom and His righteousness; then all these things will be given to us as well.

UNEQUALLY YOKED IN BUSINESS

For the longest time, I believed that you could only be unequally yoked in marriage. The business world was different, so I thought. Well, in one sense it *is* different in that if you are an employee of a company, it's not only acceptable to work for and with nonbelievers; it's almost impossible not to do so. On the other hand, if you're starting your own company as I did, I would strongly recommend that your partners be believing brothers. Here is a suggestion worthy of following: Make sure that your Christian brothers are going to be excellent partners in every possible way. Being a Christian does not automatically make you a good worker or a good partner. I know this from experience.

When I went into business with my two partners, we got off to a very good start. But it wasn't long before they began to dislike the fact that I was a Christian. I didn't shove my beliefs down their throats or put them down in any way. One Christmas we had a company party, and each partner was going to say a few words. When my turn came, I simply referred to the gathering as a Christmas party and thanked God for everyone there. I then asked if we could say grace, which I led. Virtually every employee later thanked me for my words and for the prayer. They said we needed more of that.

But my partners and their wives were infuriated

with what I had said. The next year they confronted me, telling me that I wouldn't be permitted to do that again. When I asked them why, they told me they had received a number of complaints from our employees. I thought that was odd since virtually all the employees had told me how much they appreciated it. Then I asked them who had complained so that I could go to them and apologize personally. Naturally, they said they couldn't give me the names because it was "confidential."

From that moment on, the partnership was headed downhill. My vacation time was challenged. My workload was challenged. Even what I did with my vacation time was challenged since I was using much of my vacation time to travel throughout the northeast preaching at lay renewals.

It Could Have Been Different

At the beginning of this chapter, I said it might have been different had I known then what I know now. What I didn't know was the true power of prayer and blessing. I didn't understand that I was a businessman who had authority in the heavenlies to overcome this situation. You see, I never blessed those two men. I never prayed peace upon them and our employees. I never prayed for their felt needs because I rarely fellowshipped with them since they were "the lost." In essence, I used them just as they used me. How? By doing what was necessary to build a successful company. I thought it was important to make the company a success so that A.J. and I could give away large sums of money to important causes. And we did just that. My wife worked with the homeless and unwed mothers, while I preached. We supported our church, Young Life, and many other worthwhile ministries. We even became involved with these ministries personally. We helped our parents and siblings. We gave away 25 to 40 percent of our income. But look at this carefully: During that entire time, only two people in our company came to Christ. And praise God they did!

What's Wrong With This Picture?

It's simple. I had little compassion for the lost— no vision of reaching the marketplace for Christ. I didn't realize that God had placed me in this situation to be an agent of change for my company and others. I thought my calling was twofold—first, to equip the saints, and second, to make money to support the kingdom. I was working in New York City with great men of God like Ben Patterson; David Bryant, founder and president of Concerts of Prayer; Bob Bakke of the National Day of Prayer; Hal Rich, a Wall Street COO and head of a ministry called B.O.L.D.(Business Outreach Lord Directed); and Roger Wilkin, regional director for Young Life. We were seeking God's face for revival in New York City. Yet in my estimation, I never reached my full potential as a Christian businessman. I never fulfilled my calling. No one ever told me that I was called by God as a businessman. Even though my hero was Jeremiah Lamphier, the New York City businessman responsible for the 1857 revival that began through prayer, I had little compassion for the lost.

You see it was wrong of me to go into business with two unbelievers, but it wasn't unsalvageable. Had I recognized my calling as a Christian businessman and followed the biblical principles of prayer evangelism (see *That None Should Perish* by Ed Silvoso, Regal Book, Ventura, C.A.) it might have been different. My partners might have come to know Christ. Clients might have come to know Christ. People might have been healed of wounds and illnesses. Lives might have been changed dramatically. Our company might have been seen as a truly Christ-centered company. We might have been able to sustain our business and become extraordinarily successful. I really wanted this to occur, but by the time I split with my partners in 1989, it was too late.

If you find yourself "unequally yoked" with business partners, you shouldn't automatically think about breaking up the relationship. Seek God's face on this issue and see what He wants you to do. He may want you to begin blessing them and praying for your partners. So often we curse our unbelieving partners when we should be blessing and praying for them instead.

I'll Build a Christian Company

In 1989, I began to envision my new company—solely owned by me with no involvement from unbelievers—as a business I could build according to God's Word. Med-X was a spin-off from our original company, and it became mine when I separated from my partners. Med-X was a direct competitor of my former company, Arista.

Wanting to establish a Christian company, I began by hiring Roger Wilkin as chaplain. He was a part-time paid employee whose job was to minister to employees as they had need. Not a bad idea, except for one thing: no one ever called him for anything.

Then I created a daily morning prayer time for any employees who wanted to participate, so that we could pray for the company and any personal needs. Only my family members showed up, along with Don Dodge our computer man, who loved Jesus. I also created a weekly Bible teaching time for those who wanted to know more about God and His Word. It seemed we were well on our way to becoming a successful, Christ-honoring company.

But during this time, from 1993 to 1996, we began losing clients and eventually lost not one, but three companies. I owned Med-X, Invitel and Omega. All three companies were lost in three years. I don't know all the reasons why this happened, but I do believe one reason was simply that we had brought the church to the marketplace. "Church" meant prayer and Bible study. And while that was a good idea, it wasn't enough. It wasn't prayer evangelism, and it was only one company in New Jersey and eventually Pittsburgh, trying to make a difference in the marketplace. I'm certain there must have been others, but we never met or ministered together.

"WHY CAN'T *I* BUILD A CHRISTIAN BUSINESS?"

What was wrong in my scenario was the word "I." The Bible says that unless the Lord builds the house, they labor in vain who build it (Ps. 127:1). I never asked the Lord if He wanted me to build this company as a Christian model, nor did I ask Him how to build it. I just thought it was what He wanted and did it.

You see, the same can be said of most Christian businessmen. How many of us have actually waited on the Lord to hear His guidance on our business lives? How many of us have gone to the Lord with every business decision we needed to make? The difficulty with entrepreneurs is that we are visionaries who love to go forward with a good idea. The fun is taking a great idea and making it succeed. We don't often ask for suggestions, certainly not from God. But if God isn't building your business, who is? You won't necessarily know He is in it by the degree of success you have financially. What you will miss is all God has for you in your business—and wouldn't that be a shame?

Ultimately, I believe God had a different purpose for us than growing our business. Please understand that my competitors, all of whom were unbelievers, survived while I failed. Even my unbelieving partners are still in business. Why? Good question!

It Was All About Trust

Alice Smith, an internationally known prophetic intercessor, visited Pittsburgh the week we lost our last company. She was speaking at a conference on prayer evangelism, and I had been the Pittsburgh organizer who set up the event for Harvest Evangelism. During the conference, Alice pulled my wife and me aside and told us an amazing bit of information. She had met me at the national day of prayer that I had led prior to the conference. She told me she could not stand in my presence without weeping, so she removed herself immediately. What she had seen was tremendous suffering in my life, and it was too much for her to bear. Then God had spoken to her and told her to tell me that it was He who had placed us in the valley of the shadow of death. He said He had done this for two reasons: first, to see how much we would trust Him; second, to see how much He could trust us. Note that He was testing *us*, not just me. He told Alice that our suffering was not because of sin in our lives or bad business decisions, although I could name a long list of bad decisions and sins. By now, my bad business decisions were as plain as could be. Alice said that we were now at the edge of the valley, coming out into the light. God was pleased with us, and He had yet to do His greatest work in us.

Two things you need to know: First, Alice Smith had never met us before that day and had no idea what we were going through. Second, we were relieved to hear this because we hadn't known what to think about our situation. This was a tremendously freeing moment in our lives. We now understood that there was nothing we could have done to change the hand of God upon our lives. He had set it all in place, and nothing would change what was about to happen apart from disobedience on our part.

THE PEACE THAT PASSES ALL UNDERSTANDING

You may be wondering how we survived losing all our millions, our primary home, and our shore home, eventually selling even our furniture to make it. There's one simple answer: the peace that passes all understanding. The peace that God gives us is the only answer we can come up with. What else could it have been? I doubt we could ever have accepted losing all this had God simply asked us to do so. He did ask one rich young man to sell everything he had and give it to the poor. He couldn't do it!

I don't believe A.J. and I coveted our money since we gave away very large sums to those who were needy. But God saw something in us that He had to deal with so that we could serve Him according to His plan. When rich men hear our story, they often fear that God may put them through the same trial we went through. Don't worry about that. It will only happen if you love money more than God—or if God has a plan that requires this of you. Either way, you'll be better off with God's plan than with all the wealth you could ever gather.

OBEDIENCE IS SAYING YES TO GOD

All we did was say yes to God's call to move to Pittsburgh in 1993. We didn't know why. We just knew that Pittsburgh was where He was leading us. We never knew what God would demand of us. We just went. You need to know that once you have married and found your niche in the workplace, you must take the next step in your relationship with Christ. You must make your work your ministry and build your ministry on a holy marriage. As you become the godly head of your home, you will see your leadership and success in your work grow to even greater heights.

SUMMARY POINTS

- Success is when opportunity meets preparedness, but know that God is in both.
- Money, power, and position can each be used for good or for evil.
- If you find yourself partners in business with unbelievers, it is not an unsalvageable situation.
- If you're not waiting on the Lord regarding your business life, you are in dangerous territory.
- If God isn't building your job or business, who is?

4

So, How's Your
Marriage, Really?

I couldn't wait to marry A.J. After seeing her at the
Italian Club on that life-changing evening, I would
have married her that summer—that is, if I'd had a
job to support her and she had said yes and my
mom had allowed it. Isn't love grand? Remember,
we were almost 18, and I was convinced I knew
all I needed to know about such things. After
all, I was in love! Surely that would sustain us
through anything.

A.J. and I dated for four-and-a-half years while I
attended college and she worked as a secretary. It
was a good time for me to get to know her and for
her to get to know me. We agreed to marry right after
I graduated from college and got a job. I counted
the days until we would become husband and wife.

The job market wasn't strong in 1962, and I had
to take a position in New York City. I was to work

for the health department—not exactly a high-paying or prestigious job. When we arrived in New York, we just couldn't see ourselves living there. A.J. isn't great with directions, and she would have to take a bus, a subway, and another bus to get to work.

WE'RE GOING TO DISNEYLAND!

That was enough to send us packing for Los Angeles. Loading up our 1959 VW with all of our possessions, we headed west. Both of us got good jobs within a couple of weeks, and we settled into our new life. If you're under fifty, you probably aren't too familiar with how most marriages looked in those days. Those were the days of *Father Knows Best* and *Ozzie and Harriet* on TV. Drugs and violence were scarce in real life and on TV. We were the '50s generation, and life was so good.

We came from a generation that believed the family was an important unit, and that the husband had his role and the wife had hers. I won't try to make a case for '50s-style marriage; I'm just telling you how it was. The husband was the breadwinner, and the wife was the homemaker. He held the job, even if it took three jobs to make ends meet. She took care of the home and raised the kids. I'm not proud of this, but I've only changed one diaper in my entire life. Nor did I give the kids baths or feed them. My boys take more of an active role in raising their children than I did, and I'm glad they do. What I'm trying to say is that life was simple when we got married; we knew our roles and we lived them out.

While I am a firm believer that one parent, normally the mother, should be in the home to raise the kids, you should know that this doesn't necessarily make a marriage relationship strong and vital, nor does it make it successful. Let's take a look at what is important.

CAN A HUSBAND AND WIFE FIND UNCONDITIONAL LOVE IN THEIR MARRIAGE?

Since A.J. and I met Christ in 1977, our marriage has grown stronger each year. One of the reasons is that God has spoken to me on a number of occasions about our marriage. As I grew in the Lord, I began to hear Him speak to me more and more. It was never an audible voice, just an inner sense of awareness that the Holy Spirit was directing me. As a matter of fact, God has spoken to me about our marriage in a more compelling way than on any other subject. On four occasions, His words about my marriage were particularly dramatic, and on one of those occasions He stopped me dead in my tracks.

LEADING YOUR WIFE TO PERFECTION ON YOUR OWN

The first time God spoke to me about our marriage was while I was praying for God to change A.J. Have you ever wanted to see your wife changed so that she could become a better wife? Have you ever attempted to change your wife through helpful hints? Have you ever asked God to change your wife? Let's be honest here. I'm guilty of each of these things, and I doubt I stand alone. I'll only mention the part about my asking God to change her annoying little habits, and you'll see what I mean. Throughout much of my marriage, I actually believed that I loved my wife more than she loved me. I know now that I was wrong, but at the time I really believed it and did everything I could to make her change. Finally, I went to God with my concerns about A.J.

Before we get into that we need to recognize that we're never going to fully understand our wives. My wife has always said that she intends to remain somewhat of a mystery to me. And after 41 years of marriage, I can tell you that she's been very successful! Ed Silvoso once told our staff that he viewed our inability to understand our wives as something God built into us to keep men from becoming bored with marriage and looking for another challenge. He said that many men would become less attracted to women if we were able to fully understand them. This mystery keeps the marriage vital. All I can say is that it's worked for me. Thank you, A.J.!

OKAY, GOD, HELP ME CHANGE HER

Back to my prayers about A.J. I had been praying for God to change her for some time, and on one particular day, God entered into my prayer and it became a discussion. I was asking the Lord to make my wife more tactful, kind, and loving and God said, "How dare you ask Me to change what I have created perfectly for My purposes."

Whoa! That was a strong enough rebuke for me but God continued, "Now that you've brought the subject up, let's take a better look at you."

Oh, no, not me, Lord!

If you want her to love you more, you must

love her more."

"But Lord, You know I love her," I said doing my best Peter impersonation.

"You don't love her as much as you think, or you'd do the things she asks of you," He replied.

"What things are You talking about," I asked.

God said, and listen to this carefully, "When she asks you to do something for her, you always do it in your time, not hers."

No more questions were necessary. Bells were going off inside my mind. I knew exactly what the Lord meant. But He had one thing more to say: "Love her unconditionally, as I love you." My prayer time was over. I understood.

A LESSON LEARNED

Within a very short time, I was confronted with just what God was asking me to do. It was the Christmas season, and our company always gave nice gifts to our clients. The day the gifts were delivered to my home, there were enough boxes to nearly fill our large foyer. I was watching golf on TV, and A.J. asked me to take the boxes to the basement. My normal response is "Okay," then I wait awhile until I want to do it. That could mean days. But remembering what God had said about unconditional love, I immediately got up and took the boxes downstairs. A.J. had gone upstairs after her request of me. Soon A.J. came downstairs, and I'll never forget her question: "Jack, where are the boxes?" Had she actually forgotten that she'd just asked me to take them to the basement? No, she was simply stunned—sure something had happened to them since I would never have done something she asked so quickly. Perhaps the delivery guy had come back and gotten them because they'd been delivered to the wrong house. That would be a far more logical conclusion than that they were in the basement because I actually took them down! When I told A.J. what I had done, you could see a moment of surprise came over her face, and she gave a simple "Thanks."

I was so pleased I had listened to God and thought, *How easy this really is! How could I have missed this?* But God wasn't through with me. A week later, A.J. and I had a spat. You know the kind. It doesn't really get resolved so you remain upset with your spouse. Guess who showed up that very day? The same delivery guy with more BIG BOXES to clutter the foyer. Again, A.J. asked me to take the boxes downstairs. I sat there thinking. *Let's see how long it takes for those to get to the basement.* In other words, *I'll show her!* Ever been there, guys? Guess who showed up next? God! He reminded me to do what A.J. asked in order to understand unconditional love. While I thought A.J. didn't deserve such kindness because of our spat, it didn't matter to God. I hadn't deserved to have my sins forgiven, yet they were by the death of Christ on the cross. So up I got, and the boxes went to the basement. A.J. had been in some other part of the house so she didn't see what I'd done. When she returned she was amazed—but this time she knew how the boxes got to the basement. She looked at me and said "Thanks, Hon." It was then that she learned that God had taught me to love her unconditionally. Guess what happened as a result? A.J. returned my love unconditionally.

LOVE ELICITS LOVE

The principle is simple: Only love elicits love. Don't expect your wife to love you more unless you love her unconditionally. It works—and most of all, it's the God thing to do. "Working at love" in no way compares to loving your wife unconditionally. This changed our marriage dramatically, and it was just the beginning. What are the "boxes" in your life that prevents you from loving your wife unconditionally? Try it, you'll like it—and so will she.

DO YOU SEE WHAT I SEE?

The second time God spoke to me about our marriage, it wasn't specifically about the marriage, but about my wife's spiritual gifts. Shortly after our arrival in Pittsburgh in 1993, I was talking to my wife, and for some reason she appeared more wise and discerning than usual. I had always known A.J. could read people better than I could, but I never thought much about it at the time. As I continued to listen, I said to her, "You know, Hon, God has sure given you the gifts of wisdom and discernment since we moved to Pittsburgh." Before she could even acknowledge my comment, God spoke to me and said, "Jack, she has always had these gifts. This is the first time you've ever listened to her." As I look back it was like God was saying, "This is My daughter, and I created her as your helpmate; listen to her."

The thought fell on me like a ton of bricks. What a revelation! What had I been missing? While in

Hawaii recently, my wife and I were meeting with a well-known prophetic intercessor. He made a comment that shocked me to my senses. I was explaining to Paul how we had lost everything we had. I was sure it was God who had allowed this to happen so we could trust Him more, and that there was really nothing we could have done to prevent the losses. It was a necessary series of events that we had to go through in order to have this ministry. Paul looked at me and said, "It's easy to Monday morning quarterback any situation, but I get a sense that had you listened to Alice Jane, you might still have all your money and your ministry." That makes two tons of bricks that landed on me!

Could his words be true? Or did we have to go the route of losing everything in order to have this ministry? As he said, "We'll never know, but it might have been different." I'm so glad we have a God who redeems our mistakes as we try to follow Him. But the real question is, "Do we have to make so many mistakes?" I don't think we do if we can learn to recognize and rely on one another's gifts within our marriages. You see, it's never too late to do what you should have done years ago. We can't retrieve all that we've lost, and thankfully we've learned some amazing lessons in the process. But then again, isn't it time to pay attention?

MY WIFE HAS ANOINTED OPINIONS?

During that same discussion, Paul confirmed that Alice Jane has what he calls "anointed opinions." In other words, her opinions are often from God and not just from human thought. It didn't take 24 hours for

God to show me what Paul meant. A situation came up at one of our meetings, and Alice Jane came to me and said we needed to meet with a certain couple immediately. Not even asking her why, I knew she was right, and we asked the couple to lunch. At lunch, A.J. spoke powerfully—in a way unlike I had ever heard her speak before—making a significant point about a very important situation. *Paul was right*, I thought. *Her opinions are anointed.* From that moment on, I have sought A.J.'s opinion on everything that seemed remotely important.

The point is that we men need to recognize that while our wives may not know a thing about business, it could be that God has given us wives who have "anointed opinions," "anointed discernment," or "anointed wisdom," to compliment us in business and in marriage. Could it be that we're missing half of the equation God intends for us? Could it be that our wives could help make our businesses successful? I believe the answer is clearly yes!

THE ENEMY IS LOOKING FOR SOMEONE TO DEVOUR

Shortly after this, God spoke to me very clearly about our marriage again. It was now 1994. I was walking to the kitchen when God said, "Jack, your marriage must be stronger so that the enemy won't be able to get inside your marriage and keep you from doing what I've called you to do." I asked Him what He meant since, once again, I thought our marriage was already strong. Then God showed me what He meant using my hand as an illustration. He said, "I know you understand that when you got married the two of you became one, but you don't know what 'one' really is."

God said, "Hold out your hand and put your pointer and middle fingers together. Now look at them." What I saw was the palm of my hand facing me, with two fingers together. Then the Lord said, "While those two fingers appear as one, the enemy can get between them with any issue. He can split those fingers apart and disrupt your marriage, as well as what I've called you two to do. Here is how these two fingers must look." He had me turn my fingers so that my palm was at a right angle to my eyes. With my hand in this position, I couldn't see the middle finger since it was hidden behind the index finger. The two fingers looked just like one finger, and that was the view the enemy needed to have of our marriage. Then God said, "You must become one in all things so that you appear as one to the enemy. Then he will never be able to get in and break up your marriage or your ministry."

HAVE I GOT A PLAN FOR YOU!

The Lord also revealed that He had such a plan for us that the enemy would want to destroy us, and that the best way to destroy God's work is to come against the husband and wife. Families have been decimated in America. The enemy will use anything to destroy your marriage, too, from the children to money, from sex to your work or ministry. A.J. and I know this because Satan has tried each of these methods with us. But if you are truly one, he can find no entrance. He has no power over your marriage or work. What this means is that you must remove every form of strife, discontent, anger, even the smallest thing that causes your relationship to suffer. When you are one in Christ, you will think alike in all things. There will be no surprises. You will trust each other in everything.

The Bible says in Ephesians 4:26, "Do not let the sun go down while you are still angry." I like how the same passage reads in *The Message*: "Don't use your anger as fuel for revenge. And don't stay angry. Don't go to bed angry. Don't give the Devil that kind of foothold in your life."

ONE MORE TIME IN CASE
YOU DON'T GET IT, JACK!

Three years later, we were in financial trouble. It was the fall of 1997, and we had lost all three of our companies. I was supposed to go to Argentina as part of the Harvest Evangelism international conference on prayer evangelism. But since we didn't have the money for me to go, I decided to stay home that year. When I told A.J. of my decision, she spoke in an uncharacteristic way. Normally she's very concerned about money, yet she said, "You really need to go to Argentina." I reminded her of our financial situation, but she said it again. "You really need to go." Again I reminded her of our finances, and she repeated herself: "You really should go." For clarity's sake, I said, "Let me get this right. We don't have the money, yet you want me to go. Is that right?" She said "Yes."

We were running out of money and couldn't even make our next house payment. Yet here she was telling me to spend fifteen hundred dollars to go to

Argentina. It didn't make sense, but I listened to her anyway. At the welcome dinner for the international delegates, Pastor Omar Cabrerra was the speaker. Pastor Cabrerra said this: "If you have been having difficulty with a particular need getting answered where you live, it's probably because the heavens are like brass in your part of the world. In Argentina, the heavens are open. Try praying here and see what God does."

WE NEED A MIRACLE, NOW!

My roommate, Dr. Joe Ferrini, and I decided to pray for the sale of our house. Our house had been on the market for more than a year, and we hadn't had one offer. In fact, we were about to lose the house. Joe and I simply prayed, "Lord, sell the house! Amen." Then we went to sleep.

On Tuesday I was listening to Carlos Annacondia, an Argentine businessman turned evangelist, at the morning conference. When he finished his message, I fell to my knees and began to weep. I didn't have a clue what I was crying about, so I asked God to show me. He said, "Take care of your wife."

I said, "Lord, you know I do."

He said it again: "Take care of your wife."

I said, "Lord, you know I do."

He said, "Take care of her better, and take care of your kids."

I said, "Yes, Lord," and immediately stopped crying and got up and went on with my busy schedule.

At 10:30 P.M. Joe and I were at an evening session in an arena some five miles from our hotel. I was tired and asked Joe if he minded going back to the hotel. He agreed, so we headed for the bus that transferred the delegates to the hotel. As we left the arena, I saw a popcorn vendor, remembered how good their caramel popcorn is in Argentina, and stopped to buy some. What's the point? You'll see. God is in the little things; His timing is perfect.

After buying the popcorn, we took about twenty steps and ran into Ray Llovio, another Harvest staff member. He asked if he could join us, and I said he could since there were plenty of seats on the bus. As it turns out, Ray didn't have any money with him and wanted to take a taxi. You see, Ray has a ministry to cab drivers. He's brought more than a hundred drivers to Christ during one of these 10-day conferences. It would be no different this time. So Joe and I got in the back, and Ray jumped in the front and began to engage the driver in Spanish while we ate our popcorn. We arrived at the hotel at 10:50 P.M., and sure enough, the cab driver wanted to receive Christ. We prayed for him and got out of the cab.

Joe pointed out a telephone store from which he'd called his wife a few days before. He offered to pay for me to call my wife. I had never called her from Argentina because it was always so expensive and difficult. I agreed, and we went into the store and I called my wife. When she answered the phone, she said, "Where have you been?"

Dumbfounded, I said, "In Argentina, where you sent me. Why?"

A.J. said, "I've been trying to find you for two days. I've called your hotel and Harvest, and no one can find you. Where have you been?"

I asked her what was so important, and she said,

"On Sunday a man came to see our house (that would be the day after Joe and I prayed our simple prayer, "Lord, sell the house!"), "and he has made us an excellent offer. But he needs to have your written approval of the price, or he'll go to the next house. He needs it by tomorrow morning." I told her I would send a fax as soon as we hung up.

When I came out of the phone booth, I saw that the owner of the store had everything closed up tight. He couldn't understand English, and yelling didn't help at all. But God had another surprise for us. A couple from the conference were in the next phone booth. When they came out, we learned that one of them spoke some Spanish. She talked the store owner into letting me send my fax, and the house was sold.

Wives Just Seem to Know These Things

Why do I tell you this story? I can't explain it, but Alice Jane had just known I needed to be in Argentina. It was not the logical thing to do, considering our financial situation. It was totally contrary to how she normally would have responded. The only thing I can say is God speaks to Alice Jane. Paul is right; she has "anointed opinions." If I hadn't listened to her, we may have had to declare bankruptcy. Instead, while we lost everything, we never had to declare bankruptcy.

Listening Is a Gift

By the way, remember the "Take care of your wife better" point God was making? Immediately after I hung up from talking to my wife, I knew I had to return home on the next plane. Over the next twenty-four hours, many people heard about our situation and the sale of the house. Women came up to me in the hotel and at the airport as I was getting ready to board the plane. Each one told me the same thing, "Whatever you do when you get home, don't talk. Just hug her and listen." At least ten women told me the same thing! I guess God knew I needed to hear it more than once so that I would actually do it. When I got home, my wife explained to me—because I was listening and not talking—that the loss of our house was like a death in the family.

Now guys, please don't try to figure this out. Most men would never see it that way. However, every woman I told not only understood it but began to cry herself as she felt Alice Jane's pain. If you really trust your wife, sometimes it's best to just be quiet and take care of her. I had to allow my wife to process this "death" over a long period of time and not question her about it. That, I learned, was part of "taking care of your wife better."

MORE BOXES

Remember the story of the boxes? Well, those were minor compared to the boxes I would move out of our foyer over the next two months. God had two purposes for the boxes. The first purpose was to teach me unconditional love. His second purpose was for me to keep the house orderly while A.J. packed the moving boxes. I was never much help around the house prior to this, but every time the foyer began to get crowded, I would pack the boxes in my car and take them to my mother's basement.

You see, for my wife, that too is a big part of "taking care of your wife better."

YOU CAN HEAR FROM GOD

I am convinced that every follower of Christ can hear from God. When God begins to move in revival and awakening it's because He is speaking to His people and they are listening and obeying Him. The way to ushering in a great move of God is to develop your listening skills regarding your marriage. Ask God to speak to you about your marriage. When He speaks about your marriage, He will also begin to speak to you about your work. Eventually your ears will be trained to hear Him talk about the great move He has planned for us in this generation. Once God has His people paying attention to Him in their marriages and jobs, He will begin to tell us what His plans are for the city and world.

SUMMARY POINTS

- God has created your wife to fulfill His purpose.
- Love your wife unconditionally.
- Your wife is a gift from God, and she is gifted.
- The enemy is looking for someone to devour, and he often targets marriages
- Take care of your wife—better!

MERE ASPECTS
OF LOVE:
RATING MARRIAGE FROM
ONE TO 10

I'm not much on marketing research information when it's supposed to apply to the entire country or world. People are different. So whenever you hear that "people like this" or "people want that," there are always exceptions to the rule. I'm sure what you are going to read here will be no different. I present it to you because I happen to believe that this information about American marriages is quite accurate. I have tested it myself with similar results.

A Christian research organization took a survey of married couples, asking them to rate their marriages from one to ten, one being the worst and 10 being the best. They were in the same room when the question was asked. In each case, the husband went first; almost without exception he would answer with a strong "10," while his wife would simply say

"2." When the husbands heard their wives answer, they were dumbfounded.

"How could that be? How can you think our marriage isn't a 10? I mean, it's at least an eight—isn't it honey?"

"No, it's a two," she would respond.

"Well, certainly you mean a six or a five. It can't be lower than a five, can it, sweetie?"

"No, it's really a two, dear."

This scenario is far more common than you might think. But how can two people living together have such a disparate view of their relationship? One reason is that we really don't understand each other's needs. We think we do, but we really don't. Instead, we operate out of our own needs and experiences, and treat our spouses the way we want to be treated. That just won't work.

GIFTS OF STONE

Two stories about gifts I gave my wife early in our marriage will help you understand how little a newlywed young man—or even an older married man—really knows about the woman he married. My first story is about a Mother's Day gift. We had only been married a few years, and my wife had an old Pontiac LeMans. It was costing us a lot of money to maintain, but since we couldn't afford a new car, we had to keep this car running. It was Mother's Day, and I had a gift in mind that I thought would be perfect for A.J. I went out and bought my wife four brand new tires for her car. Her tires needed replaced desperately! But A.J. wasn't too pleased with the gift, and she told me so. I thought she would see the practicality of my gift, considering our situation. What I learned in a hurry was that a box of candy would have been better than four tires, a battery *and* a tune up! Why? Because A.J. doesn't care about cars. They are a necessity to her, not a gift. And certainly not a Mother's Day gift.

My second story takes place during the Christmas season. One December as I listened to the Christmas commercials, I learned something very interesting. There are after-Christmas sales that offer tremendous savings. Why, you can save 50 percent or more on the same items you might buy before Christmas! My wife loves to go shopping the day after Christmas because of these tremendous sales. So if this gift doesn't make sense, I don't know what does: I decided to take 100 fresh dollar bills, wrap them in a box, and put them under the tree. I couldn't wait until she opened the gift. But after seeing her face when she saw those bills, I was sorry I was there when she opened it. Once again, she was disappointed. I learned she'd rather have a $100 in gifts that I had chosen than $200 in gifts she could select herself. It's the caring that counts, not the size of the gift.

Are you getting the point here? Men are often so practical that we lose sight of our wives' needs. You see, we really don't know our wives like we think we do.

WHAT ARE YOUR NEEDS IN MARRIAGE?

A recent survey of husbands and wives asked them to list the top issues that concerned them in their marriages. Here are the top five needs listed by men and women.

MEN	WOMEN
1. Sex	Affection
2. Recreational companionship	Conversation
3. Attractive Spouse	Honesty and openness
4. Affirmation (support)	Financial security
5. Admiration	Family

Sound familiar? Our needs are truly different. None of the top five needs appears on both lists. As I look at my own marriage, the top five listed by women are indeed important to my wife. For me, three of the top five listed by men are important. Affirmation is vital to me, but I want it coupled with honesty coming from my wife. At a recent Harvest ministry meeting, Ed Silvoso spoke to the women in the room saying this, "Women, you need to know that men need affirmation about their ministry or work. Affirmation is very important to men. The problem is most women think that if they affirm their husband in his work or ministry, he'll work even more than he does now—and he already works too much!" Ed said this is not normally what happens. Most husbands want to be affirmed by their wives more than by anyone else. If a man is affirmed by his wife, he'll want to be home even more. You see, if a man doesn't get affirmation at home, he will get it elsewhere—and that's not where it needs to come from.

MERE ASPECTS OF LOVE

If you look at the men's list of needs, you'll see that three are about the physical aspect of life: sex, recreation and attractiveness. With women, only financial security is not about relationship. Could it be that the top four on the men's list are driven by our need for admiration?

Notice that "love" does not appear on either list. Men typically think that sex is love, while women equate affection with love. Neither quality is in fact love; both are merely aspects of love. As we learned earlier, God thinks differently about love than men and women do. God says that despite our personal needs, whether they appear on the preceding survey or not, we're to love one another unconditionally. Then all else will fall into place. Every form of love God speaks of in Scripture is an important part of life, but unconditional love is for a lifetime. It truly changes life when it's applied to a spouse. I can tell you from experience, many issues fade in importance as you grow older. But some issues become more important as we begin to really know one another.

KNOW WHERE YOU STAND

Here's the key to the first survey, in which couples ranked their marriages from one to ten. While we all should be striving for a 10, the most important thing is that, as a couple, we can agree on a number that honestly reflects our marriage. It doesn't matter whether it's an eight or a two. But it *does* matter that we both agree about the number. If you and your spouse agree that your marriage ranks below a five, you'll be able to work on it from the basis of unconditional love. From there, you can move forward.

I'm not saying we should stop trying to figure our spouses out and simply rely on unconditional love to cover all our differences. That won't work. We need to get to know each other more and better. It will take time, energy, and lots of prayer—but it's worth it. It's a must if we're to follow God into our complete calling. Whatever you do, don't get complacent about your marriage. Don't take your wife for granted. Make your marriage the most important relationship you have, apart from your relationship with God. It will take time, effort, patience, kindness, concern, and above all love, real love. Remember, God knit your wife in the womb of her mother, and she is a gift.

YOUR WIFE IS A GIFT ON LOAN FROM GOD

It was my pastor in New Jersey, Ben Patterson, who told a group of men at a marriage retreat that God gave us our wives as gifts on loan. Now, there may be times when you feel like returning her, but God gave her as gift and, when He receives her back, He wants to see her better off than when He gave her to you. The times when you feel she's not the gift you had in mind are the times when you need to remember to love her unconditionally.

It's like the story of the farmer who invited his pastor over to his farm for dinner after church. Following dinner the farmer took the pastor on a tour of the farm. As they were returning for dessert, the pastor said, "Isn't God's creation beautiful? What a Creator!"

The farmer said in a matter-of-fact tone, "You should have seen what it looked like before I put my hands to work on it."

While the land was beautiful when the farmer bought it, the farmer had made significant improvements. The land, on loan from God, was returned in better condition than when the farmer got it.

God created your wife in His image, and He gave her to you. Think of that for a moment: God gave you one of the special creations He loves, and He wants the best for her life. He's entrusted you with His loved one. How will God see your wife when she's returned? How does He see her now? The same? Worse? Better? It's very important to Him, and it should be equally important to us as husbands.

Being a Christian businessman is different than becoming a godly businessman, and becoming a godly businessman begins at home in your marriage. Believe me, you don't want to leave home without a solid, Christ-centered marriage that is operating in complete unity. If you do, you'll never reach your full potential as a godly businessman. You can't do it without God, and you can't do it without her.

I am fully persuaded that if we are going to see a great move of God in our day, it will require that we understand unconditional love. Toward that end, we must begin by learning about it with our wives. From there, we'll be able to love the world and see God move in our workplaces and our communities.

I don't know about you, but one of the main

reasons I wanted to make a lot of money was to give my wife and kids all they needed or wanted. But that's what *I* wanted. Have you ever discussed your career with your wife, to find out if you both see it the same way? Maybe it's time to do just that.

SUMMARY POINTS

- God has given you your wife as a gift on loan, and He wants her back in better condition than when He gave her to you.
- We need to better understand our wives in order to have godly marriages.
- Husbands almost always rate their marriages as stronger than their wives rate them.
- Men equate sex with love, while women think intimacy is love. Both are merely aspects of love.
- The practical way many men think often limits our ability to understand our wives' needs.

6

THE JOY IS IN THE JOURNEY, BUT WHERE DID SHE GO?

Every time I hear a Christian talk about what's important in his or her life, it's the standard answer: God is first, followed by family, then work. It sounds good, but everything we see and read suggests something different. Statistically speaking, divorce rates, adultery, sexual problems, lack of work ethic, and countless other problems are as high among Christians as among unbelievers. The way I see it, there are only two possible answers. Perhaps God and family are not really in the one and two positions— or perhaps, God and Christianity really don't make a difference in life.

If the second answer is correct, then we're all in trouble. I don't think any of us who truly know Christ as our Lord and Savior would agree that God and Christianity don't make a difference. We've seen God move in other lives, as well as in our own. That being the case, the responsibility must fall upon us and us alone.

THE ENEMY IS US

I was living in New Jersey in 1993 when the World Trade Center was bombed by Muslim extremists. I remember the time period well because I often had to fly out of Newark or Kennedy airport on business. The day after the bombing, both airports, plus LaGuardia airport, had barricades everywhere. At Newark you couldn't park near the terminal, making it a terribly inconvenient time to travel. You also had to arrive at least two hours before your flight just to get through security. When you boarded the plane, you looked around for anyone who might look like a terrorist.

Later there was the bombing of an Oklahoma City federal building in which many Americans were killed. Immediately, we all knew it had to be those Muslim extremists again. But everyone was quite surprised when we learned that the terrorists were in fact American citizens. A newspaper headline read, "We found the enemy and the enemy is us."

Could it be that we Christians are the reason why God and Christianity don't appear to be making a difference in our marriages or society? Could it be that the reason we seem no different from the lost is that we don't practice what we hear or say? James 1:22-25 says that we are not to merely listen to the word, but we're to do what it says. If we don't do what it says, we are deceiving ourselves. However, if we take what we have heard and do it, we will be blessed in what we do.

Is God number one in your life? Then act like it.

Are your wife and kids next? Then do what you can to demonstrate it. Is your career last on the list? Great, but remember, it's also your ministry.

WHAT'S FIRST IN YOUR LIFE?

How would you ever know what's truly first in your life? It's simple. The Bible says, "For where your treasure is, there your heart will be also" (Matt. 6:21). This verse is preceded by the command, "Do not store up for yourselves treasures on earth, where moth and rust destroy, and where thieves break in and steal" (Matt. 6:19-20).

I like the way Eugene Peterson expresses these verses in *The Message:* "It's obvious isn't it? The place where your treasure is, is the place you will most want to be, and end up being." Listen to how *The Message* expresses Matthew 6:25–33:

> If you decide for God…it follows that you don't fuss about what's on the table at mealtimes or whether the clothes in your closet are in fashion … Has anyone by fussing in front of the mirror ever gotten taller by so much as an inch? All this time and money wasted on fashion—do you think it makes that much difference? … What I'm trying to do here is to get you to relax, to not be so preoccupied with getting, so you can respond to God's giving…. Give your entire attention to what God is doing right now.

In other words, *put God first!* If your treasure is

success or wealth, you need to know that's the place where you'll focus your time and energy. Success is a poor substitute for God and a failing source of significance. Jesus doesn't oppose wealth or success, but He is opposed to misplaced passion. These verses tell us that God wants us to have a single-minded devotion to Him, and all else will spring from that devotion. If you focus on God, sin will melt away and be replaced by peace, joy, and love. If your passion for success or wealth is greater than your passion for God, you are in a dangerous place.

Matthew 6 sounds a lot like the way my friend in Ghana lives his life—not fussing in front of a mirror or wasting time and money on fashion. Instead, he is more concerned with God's giving and knowing what God would have him wear that day.

SERVING TWO MASTERS NEVER WORKS

Jesus said this: "No one can serve two masters. Either he will hate the one and love the other, or he will be devoted to the one and despise the other. You cannot serve both God and Money" (Matt. 6:24). Jesus didn't say you can't serve God and *have* money. He said you can't *serve* both. There is a big difference between the two. Many wealthy business people serve God in amazing ways.

IT'S ALL ABOUT YOUR PRIORITIES

The question still remains: How do I know that I'm in line with what Jesus was saying? It's all about priorities in life and how you spend your time. In my life, my priorities are measured by the time I spend doing something. From 1964 until

1977, I spent a lot of time golfing. I would get up at 4:30 A.M. on Saturdays and Sundays to get in my eighteen holes. I never got home before 3 P.M. When I did get home, I was too tired to do anything except lie in front of the TV and watch—you guessed it—golf. On the weekends we even began to have dinner after 6 o'clock so I wouldn't have to miss the end of a golf tournament. I also played golf once or twice during the work week. On some occasions a friend would call me to play a game of golf and A.J. would schedule it for us. So, I worked five days a week, played golf at least two times during the week, and watched golf on TV.

What were my priorities? Work and golf. God was nowhere to be found in my schedule, and Alice Jane placed a very distant second. Did I do this because I was unhappy at home? Absolutely not. I loved being home with my wife and kids, but after climbing the corporate ladder and playing golf, what real time and energy did I have left? My only daughter Kristin might say about someone like me, "What can you expect? He's acting just like an unbeliever. That's what unbelievers do. They're sinners. They don't know any better." She is perfectly correct. Unbelievers don't know any better. But believers should, shouldn't we?

My wife and I were unbelievers during this time, and both of us thought we were doing the right thing. A.J. will tell you she supported me in my drive for success. She wanted the big home and all that success would bring. You see, we were truly equally yoked at this time in our lives. She didn't care if I golfed. However, when I gave it up because the kids were active in sports and I needed to be at their games, she realized how much time it had been taking. So did I.

I LEARNED THE HARD WAY

Once I met Christ, I can't tell you how many times I questioned my own motives about the quest for success I had built into a monument. There were many times when I wanted to chuck it all and get a job that would give me the time I wanted for God, my family and me. I remember asking one of my partners, "Will there ever be a time when you have all the money you want and all the time you want? When you have a lot of time, you don't have any money to do anything. But when you have a lot of money, you don't have the time to enjoy it! Will you ever have both?" He just laughed and said, "Probably not."

If that's true for most of us, then what is most important to us?

WHAT DO YOU HOLD DEAR?

A great lyric from Graham Kendrick's song, "All I Once Held Dear," really puts who we are and what we need in proper perspective.

What do you hold dear? What are you building your life upon? What do you count as gain?

If it isn't Christ, it isn't worth it. There is no greater thing. If you want to know what is truly important, consider what will matter ten thousand years from now.

Do you remember about two decades ago when in most families both the husband and the wife were climbing the corporate ladder, and psychologists were attempting to determine the impact on children? Someone came up with the statement, "It isn't the quantity of time that's important; it's quality time." How absolutely ludicrous that statement is! My pastor, Ben Patterson, had a better statement: "Love is spelled T-I-M-E." The same applies to marriage and our relationship with God. The time we spend must be sufficient and full of quality.

Could it be that many of us have attempted to fit our wives into an already crowded life, in which success is the goal? Are we satisfied with what we think is quality time with our wives since it's all we have left in the day? Are our wives as satisfied as we are?

The real question is: Is this race for success the "for better" or "for worse" part of our marriage vows?

IT'S CALLED SACRIFICE

A good friend of mine is Rick Newton, a businessman who works for a successful company just outside of Pittsburgh. The owner of Rick's company has a unique policy that allows each employee to determine how much money he wants to make each year. The employees are permitted to select the number of hours they want to work—30, 40, 50 hours per week, or more. Their pay is reflected by the number of hours they work.

Rick has decided to forsake a large salary and work forty hours each week so he can serve his family and the Lord. He has taken a 25 to 50 percent cut in pay to serve God and his family. This was not an easy decision for Rick since he has had numerous prophetic intercessors pick him out of the crowd and tell him that God was going to make him a millionaire. In today's world, you can't do that by working just 40 hours each week. At least that's what the world says. Rick believes the Lord will do what He wants with him if he seeks first the kingdom of God. I agree. In the meantime, Rick is achieving a balance many men desire but never attain.

Few men, let alone Christian men, ever start out planning to crowd out their wives in the pursuit of success. We don't do this with malice of forethought. That was certainly never my plan. But somehow, some way, it just seemed to happen. All I wanted was to be married to Alice Jane, have kids and be successful. Who knew what it would take? Issues come up that moderate our plans. Jobs become more important than we intended. Success seems just a step ahead of us— and when we achieve it, we have to maintain it. Was there ever a time in history when this wasn't the case? I doubt it. Human nature is to fall for what the world offers us and consider it good.

Please know that success and money are not the real issue. The issue is how much you will sacrifice to achieve them. Are you willing to sacrifice a close relationship with your wife and perhaps even your marriage for success? Something always enters into married couple's lives to cause separation. Unfortunately, it's often at least one partner's career.

SACRIFICE IS FOR THE ADVANCEMENT OF OTHERS

It's fairly clear that we in America are too selfish to sacrifice ourselves in order to properly care for our children. Webster's dictionary defines *sacrifice* as: "The surrender or destruction of something prized or desirable for the sake of something considered as having a higher or more pressing claim." If you like baseball, check out this definition: "A sacrifice bunt is a hit that enables a runner on base to advance, while usually resulting in the batter being out at first base." In other words, to sacrifice is to give up something you prize or that is valuable to you. God gave up His Son for us—His one and only Son—so that generations of people could know and follow Him.

This reminds me of a woman who was preparing to serve as a missionary in Africa. It was her lifelong dream and her destiny, she thought. She spent years sacrificing and preparing for her calling as a missionary. But just as she was about to leave for Africa, she learned that her sister had died, leaving her four young children without a parent. Guess what happened? This woman, who was ready to fulfill her lifelong dream and calling, decided she needed to care for her sister's children. So, she put her plans on hold and went to be with the children. She never did become a missionary. But listen to how the story ends. Each one of her sister's four children became missionaries and went to Africa.

Here is the point of this true story: Sacrifice is for the advancement of others. While this woman resigned her dreams completely, God made it four times better. Her true calling was to prepare four others for the mission field, not to go to Africa as she thought. I can't imagine how the woman felt when she made that huge sacrificial offering. She may have been confused or angry at God for taking both her sister and her dream. But can you imagine how blessed she must have felt as God began to reveal the full picture to her piece by piece?

YOU DON'T ALWAYS CHOOSE TO BE SACRIFICIAL

Sacrifice isn't always deliberate in nature. In other words, sometimes we don't make the decision to give up something for the good of someone else. Sometimes we do it with great joy, but other times we don't really know we are laying down our lives for someone else. We think we will just have to delay our desires for a moment. Regardless of how we approach sacrifice, it ultimately works out the same way: your life for that of another. Just ask Jesus; He made the decision to give up His life, but first He went through a very difficult time. He was so filled with stress and anxiety that He sweat droplets of blood as He asked the Father to remove the cup He was about to drink. But in the end, He knew what he had to do, and He did it.

In light of all this, would you as a husband be willing to give up your life for your wife? Would you be able to abandon your dreams for your career, in order to create a home environment that is conducive to holiness? Is your wife more important than the desires of your heart?

It's the Flesh

This decision is more about the flesh—original sin and the world we live in—than about the devil. I've found that there's little the devil needs to do when we're messing up our lives all by ourselves. I'm not saying that the forces of evil are totally absent in these situations, but I never personally encountered the enemy's interference until my wife and I got serious about following God, reaching cities for Christ, and building a Christ-honoring marriage.

What does that say about us? Well for starters, we live and work in a fallen world. We also tend to like the world and what it offers more than we like what God offers. Is that true of you? We can only answer for ourselves. Are you comfortable with the earthly life? What drives you to seek great wealth and success at the expense of the ones you love? Is it just the game that you enjoy?

More and more men today are questioning their motives regarding money, success and position in the marketplace. Those who love the Lord are beginning to wonder why God has put them on earth, or why they are in the place where they are. That's a real breakthrough. Often we make our own dreams come true, but then find them empty when they are realized. By the time we successfully climb the corporate ladder, we realize it's leaning against the wrong building. We may have lost a family through divorce or separation. We no longer understand our spouses as we did when we were first married. The flame of love is down to a flicker. The woman we married and loved has been left in the dust.

WE ARE IN A WAR

Ed Silvoso once told me that situations like this often occur because we don't recognize that we're in a war. We think it's normal to have broken relationships— like one of those things in life that just got away. But the true cause of our losses is that we have spiritual strongholds that need to be removed. A spiritual stronghold is Satan's secret weapon. Ed's definition of a spiritual stronghold is "a mindset impregnated with hopelessness, that causes us to accept as unchangeable the situations we know are contrary to the will of God."

Do you see your marriage as hopeless and unchangeable? If you do, you need to know that it's not hopeless. It is not unchangeable. But divorce is definitely contrary to the will of God. You need to know this because the enemy stands ready to destroy any marriage in which he is given room to work. Why? It's simple. When your marriage is in trouble, how much time do you have to grow in the things of God? When do you have time to follow God?

Where are you regarding this issue? When we turn from our wicked ways, seek God's face and pray, things will change. God promises that He will hear from heaven and heal our land (2 Chron. 7:14). In this case, our land is Christian marriages. Yes, He can heal *your* marriage too. Nothing is impossible for God.

Don't let the enemy get into your marriage. Keep it healthy and holy, as God intended it. Tear down that stronghold in your mind, and when you do, you'll be free to begin to build your marriage on a biblical foundation that will become the true foundation of a great move of God. Your ministry in the marketplace will be enhanced through your marriage.

SUMMARY POINTS

- We can't leave our wives in the dust while pursuing our careers.
- If God and family are not your main priorities, your Christianity will have no appeal to the lost.
- What do you hold dear and build your life upon?
- Is your race for success the "for better" or "for worse" part of your marriage vows?

7

HUSBANDS, DON'T LET YOUR PRAYERS BE HINDERED

Reaching the marketplace for Christ requires tremendous prayer. Being a godly worker in the marketplace requires a tremendous marriage. But what if your prayers are being hindered *because of* your marriage?

First Peter 3:7 tells us that we're to treat our wives a certain way so that nothing will hinder our prayers. The word *hinder* means "to cause delay, retard or hamper." It also means "to prevent from happening." Wouldn't it be a shame to be praying daily for your business and the marketplace, only to have your prayers be hindered by the quality of your marriage? It can happen. Have you ever wondered why your prayers aren't being answered? Could it be because of the way you consider and treat your wife?

Have you ever been shocked when a Christian marriage has ended in divorce? I have, many times.

To the outsider, the relationship looked so good. How did it dissolve? Often it's because the couple didn't pay attention to how God views marriage.

As I stated earlier, your wife is on loan to you from God—and God is observing your marriage to see if she is better off, worse off, or the same since she's been with you. Paul explains in the Book of Ephesians how you can help make her better off than before.

LOOKING FOR RESPECT IN ALL THE WRONG PLACES

As the man of the house, are you living out your God-given calling as the "head of the wife" (Eph. 5:23)? Is your wife living out what God has said to her about your position in the family? To wives, God says, "Submit to your husbands as to the Lord" (Eph. 5:22). This verse is describing undeserved submission. It means that the wife must respect the husband's position as the spiritual head of the home, and therefore respect him unconditionally. But society doesn't want to hear this because today we're all equal and no man should ever rule over his wife. Society thinks that the man will only take advantage of the wife and abuse her if she submits to him. Unfortunately, most Christians believe the same thing. It's a lie, direct from the evil one.

The fact of the matter is that most men are looking for respect in many places, from sports and work to their wives and children. In the realms of sports and work, men typically receive respect by producing something that others cannot or by doing it better. Respect is earned in the world—and quite frankly, it should be earned in marriage as well. The problem men have is that they take the world's thinking into their marriages. Many men believe women will respect them if they produce worldly things, such as money and possessions. Money is important, and we all need certain possessions, but money is not what generates respect from our wives. Men who rate their marriage a "10" by the amount of money they make, will fail at securing the respect they so long for from their wives.

A GREATER PROVISION

In my opinion, while the husband must be the provider of the basic material needs of the wife and children, he must also provide something that is even more important to his family; husbands must provide an environment conducive to holiness in the home. If this atmosphere is produced through sacrificial love, respect will not be far behind.

Francis Foulkes comments on Ephesians 5:25, "Paul chooses the word *agape*, love that is totally unselfish, that seeks not its own satisfaction, nor even affection answering affection, but that strives for the highest good of the loved one. It means, not only a practical concern for the welfare of the other, but a continual readiness to subordinate one's own pleasure and advantage for the benefit of the other. It implies patience, kindness, humility, courtesy, trust and support. This love means that one is eager to understand what the needs and interests of the other are, and will do everything in his power to supply those needs and further those interests."[1]

The Word of God is fascinating in that, while it can be understood by anyone, with the leading of the

Holy Spirit and through deep study and meditation, we can often gain a fuller, more complete understanding. That's the way it is for me with Ephesians 5:22-23. While it's as simple as it reads, it's also quite complex. That's why we meditate on the Word.

This passage begins with Paul telling wives to submit to their husbands as unto the Lord. To accept this fully, we must agree that we are to submit all things to the Lord at all times. In other words, we're to give it over to Him and trust Him with it. Now, that's hard enough when you're talking about the Lord; we like being in control. But when you're talking about your husband, it doesn't seem realistic at all. How could you possibly trust him? Love him, yes—but trust him? Not in everything! God gave you a brain, didn't He? Yes—and it's to be used to figure out what God is telling you to do. Here is the crucial question: could it be that the husband is meant to present his wife to God as holy and blameless, and that if he doesn't do so, he'll be held accountable for her condition? Our problem is often that we don't read *all* the verses in this passage. By failing to do so, we fail to understand God's message. Many women read Ephesians 5:22-24 and say "No way!"—while the men are saying "Yes, Lord! Yes!" I believe God has placed the responsibility of understanding and doing these verses on each of us, but especially on husbands. I believe we need to read Ephesians 5:25-31 in full before we decide it isn't possible. But first, let's go back to Ephesians 5:21, where God says to both partners, "Submit to one another out of reverence for Christ." This verse clearly implies that the members of the body of Christ are to submit to each other, not just wives to their husbands. God has always had leaders over His people. The many kings and priests of the Old Testament were leaders. The most practical way to understand this is to realize that nothing can be led from a committee. There must always be a leader. There can only be one head of any body, and God tells us that the head of the family is the husband. He then reiterates what a wife is supposed to do in verse 22: "Wives, submit to your husbands as to the Lord."

SUBMISSION MATTERS

What does submit mean? It has many definitions, but three that apply here are obedience, humility and meekness. All three are critical in our following Jesus in all things. Why should they upset us in a marriage? In order for this to work we must act like the head. How do we do that?

Ephesians 5:25-27 tells us we are to be just like Christ. What God wants for our wives is exactly what He wants for the church of which she is a part. Christ loved the church so much He gave himself up for it. Jesus chose to die in love so that we could choose to live in love. Why? To make her holy and clean. Why? So she, the church, would be without stain or wrinkle or any other blemish, but holy and blameless when presented to him. This gives us tremendous insight as to how we are to treat our wives. As Foulkes says, "Our love should be unconditional for our wives." We've been talking about that a lot. We must also give ourselves up, as Jesus did, to see her presented to Jesus as holy and blameless.

How do you think a wife would respond to the command of submitting to her husband if her husband's heart's desire was to do all he could to prepare her to meet Christ as a holy and blameless woman? Just for your information, my wife gave a hearty amen and amen when I asked her. There is a song that many congregations sing called, "This Is My Desire." The first two lines are, "This is my desire, to honor you." How better to honor God then to honor the woman He gave you to be your wife?

Allan tells us, "The wife's subjection to the husband in light of the high ideal of unity is such that she can never find her role grievous or humiliating." I believe that our marriage will attain greater oneness the more we, as husbands, live out the practical aspects of agape love as described in the preceding paragraphs. It must begin with us being obedient to God's call on our lives as husbands.

WHY A MAN LEAVES HIS FATHER AND MOTHER

Listen carefully, man of God: The Bible says in Ephesians 5:21, "For this reason a man will leave his father and mother and be united to his wife, and the two will become one flesh."

One of the main reasons you must leave your father and your mother is to marry and prepare your wife to be holy and blameless. The reason is so that you can love your wife unconditionally. The reason is, so that you can be respected by your wife, and so that she will joyfully submit herself to you. The reason is so that your children and all the world will see what God's love can do in a marriage when the husband fulfills his God-given duty. The reason is to build up the body of Christ by building up your

wife in Christ. The reason is for you to become a
godly, successful worker in the marketplace so that
it can be reached for Christ. But there's even more
than that. The reason is so that you can be like-
minded with *your wife*, having the same love, being
one in spirit and purpose...so that you will do
nothing out of selfish ambition or vain conceit, but
in humility consider *your wife* better than yourself
...so that you will look not only to your own
interests, but also to the interests of *your wife* (Phil.
2:2-4).

Are these reasons enough for you? If not, try this
one on for size: The unity of the body begins at
home, in the marriage. A key to this is Ephesians
5:24: "Now as the church submits to Christ, so also
wives should submit to their husbands in
everything." If we look at the church today as a
whole, we would have to agree that the church is
not submitting to Christ. If it were, we would have
full-blown unity and revival, and the lost would be
won in our day as they were in the Book of Acts.

WILL HOLY MARRIAGES PLACE US ON THE VERGE OF A GREAT MOVE OF GOD?

Could it be when husbands become the true
heads of their homes, that the church will begin to
submit to Jesus Christ, and unity and revival will
reign? Could it be that this would put us on the
verge of the next great awakening? I believe it
would. Could it be that by giving ourselves up for
our wives, we will become holy and blameless as
well? A word of caution here: The wife has personal
responsibility to be holy and pure as well. It isn't

only up to the husband, but the husband is the one who must create a home environment that is conducive to holiness.

Unless we experience these verses working in our marriages, how can we have any confidence they will work with the rest of the body? How can we believe that true biblical unity in the church of Jesus Christ will ever occur? Applying these verses to our wives is critical to our marriages and will give us the confidence and faith to apply them in our jobs as well.

How Do You Begin?

Philippians 2:1-4 teaches us how to apply these principles from Ephesians. Here is what I believe God is saying to us through these powerful verses. God, I believe, is speaking directly to each of us as we begin to understand the need for unity in marriage. I know these Scriptures were intended for the church in Philippi and for the entire church of today, but they begin with a single relationship—and the most important human relationship you have is with your wife. Remember, your city will be won from your bedroom, provided that your home is in order.

It's All About Unity

To understand Philippians 2, we need to go back to chapter 1, verse 27. Here, Paul is calling the Philippians to unity and courage in the face of alien influences. This is exactly what God is telling the body of Christ today. He's saying that He wants us to be in true unity, even as the world attacks the marriage, the marketplace and His church. Why? So that the lost can be won in our neighborhoods and in the marketplace.

Let's face it: The world is coming against families and marriages in more ways than ever before. Abortion, pornography, drugs, gay marriages, living together and divorce are just a few of these alien influences. Paul raises a warning to the Philippians: "Conduct yourselves in a manner worthy of the gospel of Christ." When Paul insists on the very highest standard for a believer's behavior, he's telling us that Christians have a high calling to fulfill—and marriage is a way we express that high calling. We need to build strong marriages in order to overcome these alien influences.

FULFILLING OUR HIGH CALLING

Philippians 2:1-4 teaches us how we can fulfill this high calling. Note that Paul is not asking us to have our act completely together. He uses a small but interesting word in verse 1: *any*. Webster's dictionary defines *any* as "the least amount." Now, look at verses 1-2. If you have "the least amount" of encouragement from being united with Christ, "the least amount" of comfort from His love, "the least amount" of fellowship with the Spirit, "the least amount" of tenderness and compassion, then Paul says to make his joy complete.

Let me ask you a question: Do you think you qualify to make Paul's joy complete? It doesn't sound like you have to be a super-spiritual type to qualify. Paul knew where the Philippians were spiritually. God also knows that we're much like the Philippians. We don't *feel* spiritual enough. We don't feel close enough to God. We don't feel much compassion toward others, especially toward the lost. How can we ever be used by God?

Paul answers the Philippians and us in the very next verse, making it simple to understand how to conduct ourselves in a manner worthy of the gospel of Christ.

UNITY IS A THREAT TO THE ENEMY, TOO!

First, Paul says, "Be like-minded, having the same love, being one in spirit and purpose."

Remember that promoting unity is Paul's purpose in writing to the Philippians, so that the church will be seen in a good light. The lost see the church through our marriage too, don't they?

While I always thought that A.J. and I were on the same page in our marriage, I now recognize that we were not in unity in all things. We were not like-minded or one in spirit and purpose. In 1990, I decided to retire and go into ministry. I had recently separated from my partners, and my company was doing very well. The president of my company had been with me from the beginning, and he wanted to buy me out. But when I told my wife what I was planning, she was not the least bit pleased with my decision. All she could see was that I'd be hanging around the house, bothering her. The fact is, I hadn't been called by God to make this change. It just seemed like the perfect time for me to do what I wanted to do: full-time ministry. Remember, I never saw myself as a businessman who was already in full-time ministry.

Shortly after I announced my retirement to my

wife, I had lunch with my mentor and friend Roger Wilkin. I told him how important it was for me to retire and go into ministry, but that A.J. was very much against it. I thought I would have a sympathetic ear with Roger since he'd been a businessman before joining Young Life. Instead, Roger said something that shocked me: "Jack, don't do anything, regardless of how much you sense a calling from God, until A.J. is in full agreement." I told him I might be in my 70's if I had to wait for A.J. to agree. "Nonetheless," he said, "don't do it." Roger told me that if God wanted me to retire and go into ministry, He would be the one to allow A.J. to accept it. I knew he was right, but it wasn't what I wanted to hear.

So I didn't retire. I simply agreed to take every morning to pray and study God's Word. A.J. agreed that it would be good for me to do that.

Two years later, A.J. and I were in church, and a guest preacher, Reverend Joseph Tson from Romania, was telling about his expulsion from his native country. His story was very compelling, and it touched A.J. greatly. When he finished his message, A.J. turned to me with tears in her eyes and said, "Anytime you want to retire to go into ministry, do it." I was stunned. I hadn't been thinking about retirement for quite awhile. I was enjoying the business again and wasn't quite ready to make the change. Imagine that! God touched my wife in a way no one could have predicted, but it wasn't until 1996 that I was out of the marketplace ministry. Roger had been right. If God wants you to do something, it's critical that your wife be in full agreement—that the two of you are like-minded, being one in spirit and purpose. This book would not have been possible had A.J. and I not become like-minded and one in spirit and purpose.

Are you like-minded in your marriage and the things of God? Do you have the same love? Are you being one in spirit and purpose? If you're not, you will always have a rough time in your marriage. It will never be sufficient to support you in attaining your high calling in Christ.

CONSIDER OTHERS BETTER THAN YOURSELF

Second, "Do nothing out of selfish ambition or vain conceit, but in humility consider others better than yourselves" (Phil. 2:3). The Bible doesn't say it will be easy to do, but it is easy to understand. The first half of the admonition, concerning selfishness and vanity, is controlled by our human nature—our flesh. These qualities are common to human nature. They are natural. What we do in order to succeed in life is rarely considered selfish or caused by vain conceit. But it is, and many of us could add greed to the mix. Called by its real name, it's sin.

Selfish ambition is the root of many problems in our society. It was the problem of Jacob in the Old Testament. He wanted what wasn't his, and it didn't matter how he got it. Selfish ambition destroys our personal lives, but it also destroys our business lives and marriages. Selfish ambition brings with it wickedness and all kinds of sin. James 3:16 tells us, "For where you have envy and selfish ambition, there you find disorder and every evil practice." You can't have a great move of God when selfish ambition is the way of life. Selfish ambition hinders any move of God. We must die to selfish ambition or we will never see righteousness.

The way to put a stop to selfishness is found in the last half of Philippians 2:3. First, we must pray for God's power to change us. Then, two antidotes are needed to overcome the flesh. Humility and the ability to consider others better than ourselves will overturn the natural inclinations of the flesh. Over the past few years I've learned that there are certain areas of our lives that we just can't change no matter how we hard we try. You just can't conjure up humility. It won't work. You can't conjure up compassion either. But here's the good news: God will give to those who ask. First, ask God to show you your own foibles and failings. Then ask Him to change your heart and make you humble, so that you can consider others better than yourself. Your responsibility is to cultivate and practice the characteristics Paul speaks of in Philippians 2:3. You need to begin to act like what you want to become. It is a matter of the heart in action.

FOCUS ON YOUR WIFE'S GIFTS, NOT ON YOUR SIN

Here is an important point to remember: You are not to focus on your own sinfulness, but on the gifts and spiritual endowments that can be found in others, especially your wife. If God can have me move boxes, which were mountains for me, He can give you the humility you need to see the gifts He has placed in your wife. God showed me that the areas in my wife's life that I considered in need of change, He considered gifts. He needed to show me what He saw in A.J. Once I saw it, I could humble myself and consider A.J. better than myself. What are the areas in your wife's life that God has a higher opinion of than you do? What are the gifts and spiritual endowments you need to focus on in your wife? If you choose to focus on God and on your wife's gifts, your sin will melt away.

HOW ABOUT HER INTERESTS?

Finally, "Each of you should look not only to your own interests, but also to the interests of others" (Phil. 2:4). Without revisiting everything in the history of our marriage, I can simply say that rarely, if ever, did I consider A.J.'s interests. Now, don't confuse my caring for her, protecting her and providing for her as looking out for *her* interests. I don't know that I ever asked what her interests were, at least not at the beginning of our marriage. The fact is, I left her in the dust as I pursued my own interests. This was not intentional. I thought that my interests *were* the interests of my wife and kids. Wrong! Every marriage has mutual interests, and that's what I was attempting to provide. But that's not what Paul is referring to here.

It is critical that we introduce these basic principles from Philippians 2 into our marriages so that we can secure a foundation so solid that we can stand firm against the enemy's assaults. This will be a transformation of tremendous proportion for the church and our society, and it will not occur overnight. Those of us in the older generation and all who are married must begin to look at our marriages and rectify issues that have caused them to be less than perfect in the eyes of God. We must speak to our married children and lead them to take their spiritual positions in their marriages. We must speak to other brothers in Christ who are either married or planning on marriage, so that they can move in the right direction. Eventually, there will be two or more generations where the balance will lay in the hands of those who are leading a Christlike marriage and from there it will become the norm. We must win back the sanctity of the Christian marriage and we must start now.

OUTWARD VERSUS INWARD DYSFUNCTION

Your marriage doesn't have to appear dysfunctional to actually be a dysfunctional marriage. You can actually be doing all you know to do and loving each other a great deal, and still be missing the mark—the mark being a marriage that the enemy cannot destroy, a marriage that is so one in Christ that it is an inseparable union, a holy marriage.

So here is what we need to do as husbands and wives: We need to recognize the power of Paul's ad-monitions and begin to implement them immediately. We need to sit with our wives and talk about our individual interests. Sometimes it will be easy. I recently saw a couple on TV who were talking about what they were going to do when they finished medical school. The husband said that before they got married they made sure they had the same interests in life and asked God to show them what to do. God did, and the man and woman were planning to break ground on a new youth health center.

So, what are your wife's interests? Do you know?

Are you sure? Would your wife agree with what you're thinking? How does your wife feel about submitting to you? Does she see you as the head of the house? Why not stop now, put the book down, and find out. The person to ask is your wife. Only she knows. You may be surprised. Don't wait until you retire to find out.

Here is another good thing to do right now: Go to your wife and ask her how you have offended or hurt her. I assure you, if you have, she'll remember the offense no matter how long ago it occurred. If you've ever been told that "time heals all wounds," it was a lie. Time only deepens most wounds. The only thing that heals new or old, big or small wounds is forgiveness—and to receive forgiveness, you need to say you're sorry. So ask your wife—or ask God to reveal what you have done or said that has caused pain to your wife.

You may want to ask a few other questions of yourself and your wife. Does either one of you consider the other better than him or her? Do you consider your wife's interests as well as your own? Who is the true spiritual head of the home? Are you in unity, like-minded, one in spirit and purpose regarding your marriage—especially regarding God's calling on your marriage? What do you believe is the purpose God has for your marriage and family? Are you living it out? When you have this discussion, ask God to show you where He sees your common interests. You both may be surprised.

One major priority of your calling as a husband is your wife's holiness and blamelessness before God. So, how's your wife? If you are successful in becoming the head of your home in a godly manner, everything else will fall into place. Your work will become more enjoyable and successful, your ministry in the marketplace will be powerful, and the great move of God you desire to see will come.

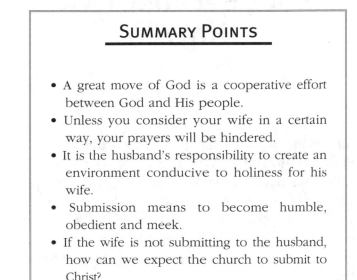

SUMMARY POINTS

- A great move of God is a cooperative effort between God and His people.
- Unless you consider your wife in a certain way, your prayers will be hindered.
- It is the husband's responsibility to create an environment conducive to holiness for his wife.
- Submission means to become humble, obedient and meek.
- If the wife is not submitting to the husband, how can we expect the church to submit to Christ?

---

1. Francis Foulkes, *Tyndale New Testament Commentaries: Ephesians* (WM B. Eerdmans Publishing Co., Grand Rapids, MI), p. 165.

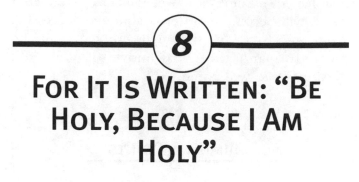

8

For It Is Written: "Be Holy, Because I Am Holy"

All we need to do is go back to the Book of Ephesians to see how to live a life worthy of the calling we have received. By applying a few simple verses, we can and ought to live holy lives. Ephesians 4:2-3 tells us, "Be completely humble and gentle; be patient, bearing with one another in love. Make every effort to keep the unity of the Spirit through the bond of peace."

Paul also writes, "So I tell you this, and insist on it in the Lord, that you must no longer live as the Gentiles do, in the futility of their thinking.... Having lost all sensitivity they have given themselves over to sensuality so as to indulge in every kind of impurity..." (Eph. 4:17-19).

Paul begins Ephesians 5 by telling us to be imitators of God and to live lives of love, just as Christ loved us and gave Himself up for us. He also tells us, "Be very careful, then, how you live—not as unwise but as wise, making the most of every opportunity, because the days are evil" (Eph. 5:15-16). And listen to this admonition: "Therefore do not be foolish, but understand what the Lord's will is…. Be filled with the Spirit" (Eph. 5:17-18). Only the Holy Spirit can lead you to be holy. Only He can help you be a true man of God who is the head of your house and a spiritual leader in the marketplace. Therefore, be filled with the Spirit.

Rather than use these verses to build a case for holiness, I want to take you to the book of the Colossians. You see, it wasn't just the Ephesians who were struggling with the issue of holiness in their lives and marriages. Adam and Eve even had a marriage problem. They never took the blame and asked for forgiveness. They each simply blamed someone else. Adam blamed the woman God had put with him for giving him the fruit that he ate; he took no responsibility for his sin. Eve, on the other hand, simply blamed the serpent, saying that he'd deceived her. If that doesn't sound like a twenty-first-century marriage, I don't know what does. Shifting the blame from oneself is commonplace today. Marriage was a common concern among the early church, and it's still a concern among the body of Christ today. It's interesting to note that Colossians 3 is devoted to two issues. First, from verse 1 to verse 17, Paul talks about the rules for holy living. Second, from verses 18 to 25, he deals with the rules for Christian households. I find it intriguing that a discussion on holy living precedes what the family is to do. You will also note that the rules for Christian households extend into Colossians 4:1;

these verses closely parallel Ephesians 5:22—6:9.

Stop and think about this for a moment: After Paul told the church how to live holy lives, he immediately turned to the family—first and foremost, to the husband and wife. Why? As I have said previously, I believe it's because the body of Christ, the church, emanates directly from the family unit. The family unit is led by the husband. What happens in the home is what builds and eventually sustains the body of Christ, the bride of Jesus.

Why is this important? Revelation 19:7-8 gives us the answer: "...For the wedding of the Lamb has come, and his bride has made herself ready. Fine linen, bright and clean, was given her to wear." Fine linen, we are told, represents the righteous acts of the saints. In other words, we must live in holiness and righteousness so that we can make the bride ready for the Lamb. Once again, this is a cooperative effort, and we must be holy as God is holy. In other words, as the home goes so goes, the church.

THE BODY WILL BECOME HOLY AND PURE

If Christian homes are filled with men who fulfill their obligations as head of the house and wives are living out their obligations as wives, we can expect to see the body of Christ becoming holy and pure. But two points of caution must be repeated here.

First, each person who knows Christ, whether male or female, is personally responsible for seeking and living out a holy life. This means that the wife must seek holiness as much as the husband. My dear friend Sergio Scataglini tells us in his book, *The Fire of His Holiness,* "The woman, too, has to assume her responsibility and understand that she is called to live a life of holiness. God is going to hold you responsible for your actions."[1]

Second, it is the responsibility of the husband to lead a holy life, lead his wife to holiness by his example, and lead his children to holiness as well. The husband must create an environment conducive to holiness in his home. Sergio tells husbands, "In terms of spiritual leadership in the home, God is not concerned about what kind of temperament you have; what your manner of thinking is; whether you are left-brained or right-brained or whether you are a person who thinks concretely. His direction is that you should assume spiritual leadership in your home. If you assume this role, it will help you avoid many disasters and conflicts in your family."[2] Obviously, if this occurs in marriage, it will flow into the body as well. This will also help you avoid many disasters in your work.

Sergio writes, "Purity is by faith. We become pure when we embrace the feet of Jesus Christ and He imparts His holiness to us. Purity is not self-discipline (although it includes self-discipline) but a miracle from heaven...the holiness of Christ can be imparted to us."[3]

JUST A CLOSER WALK WITH YOU

Abiding in Christ is the true path to holiness. Christian maturity is Christlike character. Trying the best you can to live a holy life will probably produce no fruit, because apart from Christ you can do nothing.

The Message hits the nail on the head in its rendering of John 15. Jesus says, "You can't bear fruit unless you are joined with me ... The harvest is sure to be abundant. Separated, you can't produce a thing. Anyone who separates from me is deadwood..." A few weeks ago I was cleaning up my yard, when I noticed that a vine had climbed about twenty feet up a tree. I got my clippers and cut the vine back to the ground. Just now, I looked out my office window and noticed that the vine has died and turned brown. It couldn't survive when detached from the vine that was rooted in the ground. It's now dead wood.

Jesus says in John 15 (*The Message*), "If you make yourselves at home with me and my words are at home in you, you can be sure that whatever you ask will be listened to and acted upon.... If you keep my commands, you'll remain intimately at home in my love." He adds, "I've told you these things for a purpose: that my joy might be your joy, and your joy wholly mature." It's all about relationship and being in Jesus' presence. Everything flows out of being in His presence—who we are, what we do, how we act, who we trust and everything else.

THE BODY, SUBMITTING TO CHRIST

Where does a church that is submitted to Christ come from? Certainly it comes from every man, woman and child who has received Christ as his or her Lord and Savior; but to a large extent, it comes from the Christian family that is living out a holy lifestyle. What we are about to read in Colossians will tell us how to prepare the bride of Christ for

Jesus' return. Once again, it's about holiness, marriage and the family. But before we get into the rules for holy living, we need to take a look at a topic that will help us better understand how to follow these rules.

OBEDIENCE IS BETTER THAN SACRIFICE

For a moment, let's touch upon the very important word *obedience* and its counterpart, *disobedience*. This portion of the chapter is taken from a sermon by my pastor, Donn Chapman, on the fact that obedience is more important to God than sacrifice. Since obedience is one of the three words I use to define submission, it's important that we know what God thinks about it. First of all, obedience is about how much we love God. In John 14:15, Jesus says, "If you love me, you will obey what I command." In John 14:23-24, He continues, "If anyone loves me, he will obey my teaching ... He who does not love me will not obey my teaching." Jesus is saying, *Here is how I will know you love me, by whether you obey me or not.*

In Deuteronomy 6:3, God said, "Hear, o Israel, and be careful to obey so that it may go well with you." The idea here is that if we obey God's commands, we will have His favor. I can attest to this by citing our move to Pittsburgh, when we heard God and obeyed what we heard, God poured out His favor on us and our ministry.

DOES GOD LOVE SOME MORE THAN OTHERS?

Does God love some more than others? The answer is found in Exodus 19:5, where God says, "Now if you obey me fully and keep my covenant, then out of all nations you will be my treasured possession." We can't afford to have leaders—whether they are business people or pastors—who won't obey God. If the leaders don't obey God, they will lose their blessings and the purpose God has for their lives. God loves everyone, but He loves those who obey more. Those who obey become His treasured possession. You see, you can go on with your Christian life in disobedience and lack blessings, favor and a completed purpose—or you can choose to be obedient in all areas of your life and live in full blessing, favor and purpose.

It's important to know that obedience doesn't keep the problems away; it keeps God with you so you can get through the problems. Now, that's a good reason to obey God. Obedience is hard because we each have free will, which has been given to us by God. Our flesh often overrides common sense. Even when we know we must obey God, we can choose not to do so and succumb to our fleshly desires. That, to me, is one of the main issues that prevents men from obeying God in becoming spiritual leaders of their homes; it also causes our wives to disobey God by not submitting to us. You see, if you obeyed God and lived out the position He has given you, you and your wife would become holy—and your wife would submit to your leadership. Why? Because when you are in submission to Christ, she will know it. If you obey God in this area, you demonstrate your love for God. This will translate into your loving your wife and her submitting to you.

THE RESULTS OF OBEDIENCE

The results of obedience and disobedience are found in Deuteronomy 28—a key chapter that shows how important it is to be obedient. Obedience causes God to bless your city, your country, the fruit of your womb (you children, your crops, your work), your coming and going, your battles, and everything you put your hand to. On the other hand, disobedience causes God to curse all of the above and more.

Ponder that for just a moment. Are you walking in obedience or disobedience? It seems to me that most of us have one foot on each side; we're pleased with our obedience but don't consider our disobedience that dreadful. Let's look at it from God's perspective: Our disobedience is dreadful to God, and He hates it. On top of that, through our disobedience, we demonstrate that we don't love God fully and completely.

Another result of obedience is that it can precede and produce passion. Your heart always moves in the direction of your focus, and you always focus on where your passion is placed. That being the case, obedience leads to passion, which leads to focus.

WHAT IT TAKES TO BE CALLED OBEDIENT

What does it take to obey God so that we can experience His blessings and not His curses? Let's look at seven points.

1. *Love*—This is an absolute must. We must love God and our wives unconditionally.

2. *Fear of God*—We must fear God more than we fear man. All man can do is kill your body, but God can do much more. The Bible says that "the fear of God is the beginning of wisdom."

3. *Submission*—This means that we need to become humble and meek if we're going to submit to God. What submission really means is that we will forfeit our desires for God. We will also forfeit our desires for our wife's desires. Our logic will be overruled by His Word.

4. *Discipline*—The Bible says that when we have been faithful with a few things, He will put us in charge of many things. You must work out the issues in your marriage before you can reap the fruits of your business and ministry.

5. *Patience*—"First things first" is the credo here. God has all the time in the world, and we are rarely on "God's time." We all want revival to come, but it will only come when we don't have to have it come in order to be obedient. Take care of first things first. Become obedient and watch revival come.

6. *Faith*—When you can't figure it out, faith is required. When you can figure it out, faith is required. Faith is key to all we do. Charles Stanley once said that his

grandfather, whom he had only seen four times, had a profound impact on his walk with God. When Stanley was 14, his grandfather, a preacher, told him "Faith is when God tells you to run through a brick wall and you do it quickly, knowing that when you get to the wall, God will have provided a hole for you to go through." Do you have a brick wall in front of you? Has God told you to run through it? If He has, He will provide the hole in the wall as well. Get running as fast as you can.

7. *The Holy Spirit*—Nothing I've stated above can ever happen without the presence and power of the Holy Spirit in your life. You have to have Him present in order to love, fear God, submit, be disciplined, be patient and have faith enough to run when God tells you to run. You must also exhibit all of these in order to have the Holy Spirit in your life. In short, you have to have the Holy Spirit to obey, and you have to obey to have the Holy Spirit.

WHAT ARE THE RULES FOR HOLY LIVING?

Let's discuss the rules for holy living briefly. Holy living begins with the fact that you have been made righteous through Christ and in Him alone. The issue is not works or obedience to a set of rules, but living out what you are called to be: holy and pure.

SET YOUR HEARTS ON THE THINGS ABOVE

Colossians 3:2 begins, "Set your hearts on the things above." Paul is not asking us to become other-worldly or to withdraw from work and the activities of the world. The Lord expects us to go on with our work and to maintain normal relationships in this world. The difference is, we should view everything in light of eternity. We should no longer live as if this world is all that matters. If we do this, we will ultimately have a new set of values and morals—a new way of judging things and a new sense of proportion. While we will continue to make a living in the world and use the things in the world, we will begin to use these things in a new way. If you haven't read *God @ Work* by Rich Marshall, you should pick up a copy. Marshall teaches that we must each live out our calling in the marketplace, but with a new set of spiritual eyes. If we follow what Marshall is telling us, giving will become more important than getting, serving will be more important than being served, and forgiving more important than holding a grudge. We will begin to see things as they appear to God, not as they appear to the world.

How does this happen? We must set our hearts and minds on the things above through prayer, study of the Word and fellowship with other Christians. We must have real "quiet time" before the Lord daily, and be able to become quiet at any time of the day and consider it normal. A friend of mine does what he calls a "word fast" one day a month. On a specified day each month, he separates himself from all words, be they spoken, heard or written. He gets completely quiet before the Lord and waits upon Him. The results, he says, are astounding. It has reached the point where he can't wait for that one day each month, because this is when he hears God. "Be still and know that I am the Lord," God says to each of us. Most of us don't know what it's like to be quiet before the Lord. It means what it sounds like—complete silence. It means to become contemplative. Let God speak to you in your stillness. As my grandfather always told me, "Jackie, you cannot learn anything when you are talking."

We must become holy, as our Father in heaven is holy. When we commit our lives to the things of God, we will begin to see Jesus Christ is the most important thing in life. Actually, we will see Him as life itself. You've heard it said that someone "lives for his work" or that "his work is his life." That means that a person finds all there is to life—or so he thinks—in what he does in this world. But for the follower of Jesus, Christ is your life. Jesus will dominate your mind and your heart. When you've arrived at this point in your walk with God, the world's wealth, ambitions and activities are seen for their true value.

PUT IT TO DEATH

Paul says emphatically, "Put to death, therefore, whatever belongs to your earthly nature: sexual immorality, impurity, lust, evil desires and greed, which is idolatry" (Col. 3:5). I don't think that any of these activities need clarification in any way. We all know what Paul is talking about, don't we? Romans

8:13 says it this way: "If by the Spirit you put to death the misdeeds of the body, you will live." Here is the key: We must destroy self-centeredness, personal desires and ambitions that are contrary to the will of God. Everything that keeps you from being humble, obedient and meek must be killed.

I enjoy the fact that the apostle Paul always concludes his teaching in a very practical way. Paul insists that theology must be expressed in Christian living. He makes it easy for us to apply what he is teaching us, and this instance is no different. I love Barclay's observation on this subject: "Paul begins with a vivid demand. The New Testament never hesitates to demand with a certain violence the complete elimination of everything in life which is against God."[4] The key word here is *violent*. Becoming holy is serious business, tantamount to war! Have you chosen sides yet?

RID YOURSELF OF ALL SUCH THINGS

Paul continues his emphasis on removing the things that are contrary to God's will: "You must rid yourselves of all such things as these: anger rage, malice, slander, and filthy language from your lips. Do not lie to each other" (Col. 3:8-9). Other words for "rid" are "strip," "divest" and "free." This suggests that what you are freeing yourself from is something objectionable, offensive or repugnant. The only way you can rid yourself of these things is to truly consider them objectionable. In the light of Christ, we should easily see them as evil; we should want no part of them if we are truly seeking the holiness of God.

If you need help understanding why you need to

deal with these areas of sin, just remember that the Bible says, "A man reaps what he sows. The one who sows to please his sinful nature, from that nature will reap destruction; the one who sows to please the Spirit, from the Spirit will reap eternal life. Let us not become weary in doing good, for at the proper time we will reap a harvest if we do not give up" (Gal. 6:7-9). Proverbs 11:18 says, "He who sows righteousness reaps a sure reward," but Proverbs 22:8 tells us, "He who sows wickedness reaps trouble." These admonitions should move us to want to rid ourselves of those things that cause us to fall short of holiness.

PUT ON GODLY CLOTHES

Finally, Paul tells us to clothe ourselves with compassion, kindness, and other virtues, and to become holy (Col. 3:12). I find that the best antidote to the evil caused by our sinful nature is to come against these things in the opposite spirit. Paul tells us how to do just that. After he exhorts us regarding what we must put to death and rid ourselves of, he describes what we need to do in a positive sense. Note that every one of the virtues and graces mentioned in Colossians 3:12 has to do with personal relationships. Isn't that what we've been talking about throughout this book? Marital relationships are the subject of this book. These things we are to put on will help us develop our marriage relationships, thus helping our wives become holy and pure. When this happens, the whole church will become what it has been called to become: The bride of Christ.

> Therefore, as God's chosen people, holy and dearly loved, clothe yourselves with compassion, kindness, humility, gentleness and patience. Bear with each other and forgive whatever grievances you may have against one another. Forgive as the Lord forgave you. And over all these virtues put on love, which binds them all together in perfect unity (Col. 3:12-14).

If we are willing to clothe ourselves with these virtues, we will begin to exude them wherever we go and they will touch lives in amazing ways. But again, we must begin at home. Our wives will learn holiness from us. We must shower our wives with what we have become in Christ.

Don't be boastful, self-seeking, envious, prideful, rude, angry or keep a record of wrongs. Instead, show your wife compassion, kindness, humility, forbearance, gentleness, patience, mercy, grace, faith, forgiveness, peace, protection, truth, trust, sacrifice, hope that perseveres, and above all else, unconditional love. Why? Because love never fails (1 Cor. 13:8).

WHERE MUST WE APPLY THESE VIRTUES FIRST?

Where does Paul begin these instructions regarding holiness? With husbands and wives.

Here's something else you should know about unconditional love: It's the one thing that binds all the other virtues together in perfect unity. In other words, if we are seeking unity—perfect unity—in a marriage, a family, the marketplace, or the body of Christ, we must put on love. And again, if you want to see this lived out in the marketplace and throughout the entire body of Christ, it must first be demonstrated in your marriage. Can you see how important holy marriages are to the body and ultimately to the lost? I believe that everything God is calling us to do in the marketplace and in reaching the lost will flow from holy marriages that are built on the Word of God and obedience to it. The great move of God we are anticipating is dependent upon it.

SUMMARY POINTS

- When Paul tells us how to live holy lives, he first turns to husbands and wives.
- The body of Christ becomes what the family becomes.
- The New Testament never hesitates to demand, with a certain violence, the complete elimination of everything in life that is against God.
- Becoming holy is serious business and is tantamount to war.

---

1. *The Fire of His Holiness* by Sergio Scataglini, © 1999, Gospel Light/Regal Book, Ventura, CA, 93003. Used by permission.
2. Ibid.
3. Ibid.
4. Barclay, William, *The Daily Study Bible: The Letter to the Colossians* (The Westminster Press, Philadelphia, PA), p. 180

9

WHAT COULD BE WORSE?

After having left your wife in the dust for your career it might be hard to believe that a husband could do anything worse, but some do.

BEING MODIFIED BY THE FIRE OF GOD

In the past 23 years, God has modified my personality by placing me in the refiner's fire. Most of the refining came after we arrived in Pittsburgh in 1993. Since that time, I have become quieter, more easygoing, and even somewhat shy. I like spending time alone, and I don't have to win at everything I do. I wouldn't go so far as to say that I'm an introvert, but even my wife notices the difference.

What I see happening is that I am more likely to listen to my wife and others than I did just six years ago. I'm far more reflective. Honestly, I never reflected on much of anything before because I was always looking into the future and never toward the past. God had to change me so that I could balance my focus and recognize that the past, present, and future are all important, yet none more so than the present. God tells us not to worry about tomorrow since today has enough concerns of its own. We can learn a lot from the past, but we mustn't dwell on it. Balance is the key.

I tell you all of this because we often think that once we're saved, we are a new creation. That is completely true, but it doesn't mean that we have suddenly become perfect in all ways. A friend of mine swore a great deal prior to being saved. About three days after he was saved, his secretary asked him what had happened to him. "You haven't sworn for three days," she said. That particular part of my friend's life was changed instantly. That happens to some people, but most of us go through a more gradual transformation over the years. We are transformed through prayer, study of the Word, worship, sermons, discipleship and much more. What really changes us is simply being in the presence of God. Remember how Zacchaeus was changed by being in the presence of Jesus? You can be too!

A Scout or Settler

When I came to Christ, I was no longer as concerned about success as I had been before knowing Jesus. Now, my focus was totally on knowing Jesus and desiring to grow in my new faith. Before I knew Jesus, I went after most things I did, whether work or sports, full tilt—but I never finished anything. Both of these characteristics are common among entrepreneurs and those who are somewhat visionary. But I recently heard a better description of someone like me: It's the difference between being a "scout" or a "settler." A scout is one who is out in the front, checking everything out. He always likes new things, regardless of the potential danger. On the other hand, a settler is one who likes to stay in one place, play it a bit safe, and maintain what has been built—even if someone else built it. Both scouts and settlers have a place in God's plan. My wife was concerned that I wouldn't last as a Christian because of who I was. She thought I would tire of it and move on to something else. With my history, she certainly knew the risk. But what she failed to factor in is that no one can ever tire of God and His Word. He is new every morning. I kNow, I'll always be a scout; I'll just be a better scout because of the changes God has caused in my life.

WHAT IS THE WORST PROBLEM?

Based on this, I think you may be able to see what the worst problem could be for a successful Christian businessman. Again, it's pursuing God and leaving your wife in the dust. But, isn't that okay if you're following God? Absolutely not! I believe, without question, that we are to love God more than anyone or anything in this world. But considering that God created Eve for Adam, out of Adam's rib, you'd have to believe that God never expected man to leave his wife behind as he pursued God. When God came to visit the garden, He was always looking for the two of them.

PEACE VERSUS A SWORD

Here's something else to consider: Jesus told His disciples that He had not come to bring peace to the earth, but a sword. He said, "For I have come to turn, 'a man against his father, a daughter against her mother...' Anyone who loves his father or mother more than me is not worthy of me; anyone who loves his son or daughter more than me is not worthy of me" (Matt. 10:35-37). Note that husbands and wives are absent from these admonitions. I know these verses apply to the inevitable result of Christ's coming—the conflict between Christ and the antichrist, light and darkness, and Christ's children and the devil's children. Jesus is talking about the conflict that will come within a family when one receives Christ and the others don't.

This is all the more reason to examine why husbands and wives are not mentioned in these verses. It seems to me that it has to do with two issues. First, husbands and wives are to be equally yoked. They are both to know Christ as Lord and Savior before they marry. That obviates the sword Christ spoke of bringing to Earth. Second, marriage is a choice we make. We cannot choose our children, parents, siblings or relatives. If I make the right choice in a wife, I should and must become one flesh with her. God didn't want to separate husbands and wives. He is totally against it.

ARE YOU RUNNING THE RACE IN VAIN?

So many men come to Christ and start running after Him as fast as they can. Pastor Eduardo Lorenzo is the director of Harvest Evangelism in

Argentina. The message that has impacted my life most under his teaching had to do with the race Paul spoke of as he followed Christ. Eduardo referred to Paul's race as one that required endurance and was best described as a relay race. Ecclesiastes 9:11 tells us, "The race is not to the swift." These are important definitions since most men I know, when they finally grab hold of Christ, run after Him as if it's a 100 yard dash. They see it as an individual race, and they can't wait to get to the finish line and win!

I believe we each must run our own race, as Paul says in Acts 20:24, to "complete the task the Lord Jesus has given me—the task of testifying to the gospel of God's grace." Paul was always concerned that he wouldn't do enough to make sure the gospel was proclaimed to the lost. Paul was greatly concerned about running or having run his race in vain. Are you running your Christian race in vain?

WHAT IS THE PRIZE WE'RE RUNNING AFTER?

Paul makes an interesting point when he says that in a race, all the runners run, but only one gets the prize. He tells us that we're to run in such a way that we get the prize, and that we need to enter into rigorous training in order to win. He also says, and listen to this, "Therefore I do not run like a man running aimlessly" (1 Cor. 9:26). Have you ever felt that you were running around aimlessly in your pursuit of God? I have. I've run in fits and starts for years at a time, thinking I was right where God wanted me to be, only to find out that I had missed Him somewhere along the race. I'm not saying that I didn't move forward in my faith, but it was like taking two steps forward and one step back. I'm convinced that at times I was running my race in vain. If you are leaving your wife in the dust to run the race for God you are running in vain.

A question we must ask is, what is the prize Paul was speaking about? There is no question that for Christians one prize is souls; but I don't think that is what Paul was referring to. Paul continued in 1 Corinthians 9:27, saying, "I beat my body and make it my slave so that after I have preached to others, I myself will not be disqualified for the prize." How might he have been disqualified and not have received the prize? He can't have been talking about spreading the gospel or winning souls since Paul was the consummate soul-winner and preacher of all time.

How can you be preaching the gospel, spending all your time in ministry for the Lord, seeing your business transformed for Christ, and seeing the lost come to Christ, and not receive the prize? It's very simple and clearly implied in verse 27. The prize is being in the presence of Jesus. You don't receive the prize of Jesus' presence through ministry. Why? You would be living a "works" theology. How many of us make ministry the greatest thing we can do for God? It's typical of most Christians and even more so of those who are driven to succeed and have done so in a career. We think that if we reach the lost and heal the sick, we'll get into God's presence—when in fact, it's the other way around. We need to get into God's presence to fulfill His purpose of setting the captives free and receiving His victory. We need to get into the presence of God to lead our wives, homes, and businesses, and ᴐ see a great move of God in our time.

Every pastor or businessman who spends a great deal of time in a ministry that has been given to him by God soon finds himself losing what he began with—his relationship with God through Jesus. That's the prize: your relationship with Jesus. Unfortunately, it's not long before the ministry becomes the driving force; your prayer life declines and soon becomes the last thing you do in your day—and then you don't seem to have time for it at all. Paul knew this, and he wanted to be sure he would never lose the presence of Christ in his life. He never wanted to see his relationship with Christ diminished in any way. When we lose touch with God's presence, we begin to simply do ministry the way we've done business. We take control and do it for Him. When this happens, we tend to leave our wives in the dust yet again. This results in an incomplete work and a marriage that remains unfulfilled and incomplete. It can negatively impact one's ministry in the marketplace, as well as one's level of success in a job.

WHAT'S THE SECOND BEST PRIZE WE RECEIVE?

You see, while the greatest prize is your relationship with Jesus, the second best prize is your relationship with your wife. You can't afford to lose either in your pursuit of work or ministry. Remember, these pursuits are not mutually exclusive. They depend upon one another. You and your wife need to pursue God as individuals, but you also must pursue Him together. If not, you will soon find yourselves separating, and you will no longer be one in the flesh.

ARE YOU IN THE PRESENCE OF GOD?

Please understand that my wife and I were literally thrust into the presence of God through the loss of our businesses and finances. There are easier ways to get there, but if He wants you and can't get you into His presence voluntarily, He will set up circumstances that will draw you there—unless you are totally lacking obedience. Our little bit of obedience was agreeing to move to Pittsburgh without knowing why, except that God was asking us to do so. That single step moved us deeper into God's presence. Since then, we have loved His presence and desire to stay in it. Being in the presence of God always leads to a joy that is unsurpassed. You see your job and your marriage in a better light. When this happens, ministry in the marketplace becomes pleasant and easy.

HOW DO YOU SIT IN THE PRESENCE OF GOD?

It's absolutely possible to sit in God's presence because Adam and Eve walked in the garden with God, and the Bible tells us that Enoch walked with God (Gen. 5:22). Those were amazing times for some of the first human beings that God created. Why did God walk with Adam, Eve and Enoch? I think the answer is simple: He loves what He creates, and He really loves mankind—including you and me. Out of all of creation, He only created man and woman in His image. God wanted a relationship, and He wanted it with us. The account of the creation and fall of man only takes three-and-a-half chapters in the Bible. The rest of the Bible is about God seeking us so that we can walk with Him again. Knowing this, we must believe that it is very possible to walk with God. Why? Because He wants to walk with us. Tommy Tenney would tell you that it is true worship that places us in the presence of the living God. I agree completely.

PURSUING THE PRESENCE OF GOD

Tommy Tenney, in his book *God Chasers*, writes that the reason you may not be able to win people to Christ is because "you don't have enough of the presence of God in your life. No matter what you do, without His presence, you will be 'just another somebody' to those around you." That's exactly why I'm writing this book about marriage and the marketplace. Often, Christian marriages don't reflect the presence of Christ anymore than the non-Christian marriages around them—nor do Christian businesses. Why should our neighbors and business associates want what we have? We have nothing to offer except Jesus, yet they can't see Him in our lives and marriages. Leaving our wives in the dust to pursue God dims the light in our marriages and at our offices.

God doesn't want us to chase Him by building bigger and better ministries while ignoring Jesus, our wives and our families. He wants us, as Tommy Tenney says, "to pursue His presence in our lives." He wants husbands and wives to seek His presence together, as well as alone. We must get to a point where we sense the presence of the Holy Spirit virtually all of the time. When that happens, everything will be much better, even if everything is falling apart around us Trust me, A.J. and I know of what we speak.

BE ALERT

We are told in Scripture to always be alert. Why? Two reasons are clear. The first is so that we don't allow the enemy a place in our marriages or jobs. The second is so we can hear God speak to us about our marriages and jobs. My wife's cousin Jack Yost is an evangelist. We stopped by to hear him preach one night, and his message was on drinking. The message was the best I had ever heard on the subject. He never told us that the Bible was against drinking. What he did say was that we need to be alert at all times so we can hear the Holy Spirit speaking to us. The only way we can be sure of that is to keep a clear head. Jack said that we should never do anything that will dull our minds so that we miss God's whisper. He warned us never to get involved in things that can dull the mind, like drugs, pornography, alcohol, illicit sex, or whatever temptation is specific to each of us personally. If we do, we'll miss God's presence. Remember, God is holy. You could also miss His whisper by being too busy doing ministry, doing work and lacking intimacy with Him.

I believe that at one time or another, every city has had a marketplace that was driven primarily by Christian business people. Following the awakening of 1857, cities like Washington, D.C., Philadelphia, and Pittsburgh had thousands of businessmen praying daily for at least an hour. This all happened because Jeremiah Lamphier, a businessman, was sent out by his church to be a city missionary. Lamphier started a prayer meeting that swept a large portion of the northern United States and moved overseas as well. What has happened in your city? Check it out, and I'm sure you'll be surprised. Could it be that you are being called to take up the baton of the relay race being run in the marketplace of your city, so that God can move greatly in your midst? Could it be that through your marriage, God is preparing you to do the work He has called you to in the marketplace? I think He is.

GOD ISN'T LOOKING FOR A LONER

What all this means is that we are to slow down and seek God's face about how we follow Him. How do we include others—especially our wives and children? How do you include your coworkers? You see, God isn't looking for a loner. God is looking for a husband-and-wife team to run the race together. He's looking for someone who wants to run a relay race and someone who will persevere in all he does.

We've already touched on the fact that a couple must be one in Christ and know where God is calling them as a couple. If you can agree on your calling as a couple, you have a greater likelihood of not moving ahead of one another. You won't necessarily be ministering together, but you will know what you are called to do in common and what you are called to do individually.

RICK STAYS HOME

A story about my friend Rick Newton illustrates this point well. Rick joined me on a trip to State College, P.A., where we were to meet Ed Silvoso and then speak to a number of business people. Following the meeting, Rick joined Ed and me for lunch. When you have lunch with Ed, it's often a lunch that will change your life—and that's exactly what happened to Rick. He gained a new understanding of who he was and what God would have him do. Rick took a quantum leap forward in his spiritual life.

Two months later, Harvest Evangelism was holding a City Reachers' School (C.R.S.) in State College, and Rick was planning to attend. But Rick knew that he had just grown dramatically and would probably grow even more by going to the C.R.S. That caused him to become concerned about his wife. He didn't want to go too far with God, without her having the opportunity to experience what he had already experienced. So here is what Rick did: He took a week off work and sent his wife to the C.R.S. while he stayed home and cared for their children.

One afternoon my wife was standing in the doorway of the auditorium where the City Reachers' School was being held, talking to a woman. I didn't know to whom she was talking until I got closer. It was Rick's wife, Terri. You could tell she was very moved by something; I assumed it was something she'd heard at the conference. Instead, she was telling my wife what a wonderful husband Rick was to take time off work and care for their children while she came to the City Reachers' School. She realized that Rick loved her so much that he wanted her to hear what he had heard before he could hear anymore. Why? So he wouldn't get so far ahead of her spiritually that they couldn't continue to be in agreement regarding what God was doing in their lives. Now, this is godly wisdom.

If we are going to see a great move of God in the marketplace and throughout our communities and nation, we must seek God's face together in full unity and that will begin at home. First with your wife, then with your children, and then with your coworkers.

As the husband you are called by God to be the spiritual head of the home. That means that you are responsible to create an environment conducive to holiness to exist in your home so your wife can become holy and your family can become holy. From this new base of a holy marriage you will be better prepared to see yourself become more successful at your work, and you will see your ministry in the marketplace grow. Can a great move of God be far behind if this takes place in marriage after marriage?

SUMMARY POINTS

- If you are a "type A" personality, you are probably best known as a pioneer or a "scout" and new things motivate you.
- God never expected the husband to seek God alone and leave his wife out of the equation.
- When God entered the Garden of Eden, He was always looking for Adam and Eve.
- If you're leaving your wife in the dust as you pursue God, you are running the race in vain.
- The prize Paul was fearful of losing was his relationship with Christ. What about you?

DESIRE LEADS TO PERSEVERANCE IN MARRIAGE

Prayer, obedience, love, humility, sacrifice, honesty, joy and many other elements are critical to the race we run, but unless we persevere, we can't finish the race. In chapter 9 we dealt with endurance as a critical factor in following Christ and running the race that is set before us. It's important to know that while the words *endurance* and *perseverance* have similar meanings, they are not used in precisely the same way in the Bible. While some dictionaries say that these words can be used interchangeably, they do have slightly different meanings. You can have the ability to *endure*, yet you may not *persevere*.

Let's look at the two words as defined in Webster's dictionary. *Endurance* is defined as "the ability to last or the ability to stand pain, distress, fatigue or hardship." *Perseverance* is defined as "refusing to give up; perseverance is unrelenting and persistent. It is the quality of one who persists and is steadfast, or who continues doing something in spite of opposition or difficulty."

In a study of these two words, here is what I learned: With respect to endurance, the New Testament suggests "patient waiting," but does not imply passivity. Inspired by hope, the believer finds inner strength to hold up under persecution or hardship. In other words, you stand firm in difficult situations and won't be moved. It takes a certain degree of activity to hold on and not be moved from your position, but it does not allow you to move forward.

On the other hand, perseverance in the Bible usually conveys the idea of activity. Perseverance is overcoming difficulties, moving forward by doing right. We are most familiar with perseverance as a desire to succeed at a chosen profession.

DESIRE DRIVES US TO PERSEVERE

I see these words as very similar in meaning, but one word separates them. That word is *ability*. You see, many of us have the ability to do certain things but never end up doing them. How many people do you know who are gifted in sports or intellect, but who never practice or study? They have the potential to be the best in their areas of gifting, but fail to become the best. Then there are those who have far less ability, yet go beyond the ones who are more gifted. Why is this true? I believe it happens because of one's *desire*. The definition of *desire* is "to long for." We must "long for" something if we are going to persevere.

A BASEBALL STORY

Most of us are driven by what we desire. Whatever we desire, we'll go after wholeheartedly, in spite of pain, distress, fatigue or hardship. I think of my youngest son, Jim, who wanted to play first base in Little League. Jim was 12; the team he played for already had a first baseman, who happened to be the manager's son. I pulled Jim aside one day after practice and I told him the fact of life in Little League. The manager's son, if he was a decent player, would play the position he wanted to play. My point was to warn Jim not put his heart in becoming the first baseman. I didn't want to see him get hurt. I told Jim, "Just play right field and be glad you're on the starting team!"

Have you ever attempted to protect someone from failure? Jim listened, but he didn't pay any attention to me. He desired to be the first baseman, and in spite of the opposition, he was going to pursue it. And so he did. He practiced at first every time he could and never said anything to the coach. He simply played hard.

One day the manager's son was playing first, and he made a mistake. He thought there were three outs when there were only two. He had the ball in hand, but thinking it was the last out of the inning, he ran to the dugout. While he did that, a couple of runs were scored. At that moment, his dad, the manager, came out of the dugout and yelled out to right field: "Serra, play first!" Jim had that position for the rest of the season and held it until high school. That night I told my son, "Jim, don't ever listen to me if I tell you that you can't do something. You just go for it. You proved that you can do what I thought was impossible."

You see, Jim really wanted to play first base, and he persevered. The manager's son had the ability to play, but he didn't have the desire to be the best first baseman on the team. He demonstrated this by never trying to get the position back. If you don't have desire burning in your heart, you'll never persevere in this world, let alone in the kingdom of God. I am convinced that desire begets perseverance, that perseverance allows us to finish the race, and that finishing the race allows us to win the prize.

WHAT ARE THE DESIRES OF YOUR HEART?

The desires of your heart should be to have a vital relationship with Christ, to have a vital relationship with your wife, and to have a great relationship with your work. If these are not your primary desires, and you can't seem to raise them to the appropriate level, then you need to ask God to instill them in your heart. He will do that if you're sincere in your request.

The Bible tells us that if we seek first His kingdom and His righteousness, all else will be given to us as well (Matt. 6:33). What does the kingdom of God mean? The phrase has a very wide meaning and any attempt to define it inevitably restricts its scope. In a general sense, the term means "God in control."

We are seeking the kingdom of God when we

want to see God in control of our work places, our marriages and life in general. I believe that if I seek the kingdom of God, God's control of my marriage, one of the things He will add to my life is a successful work life. We are not told to attempt to find time for God, our wives and work. We are told to seek the kingdom of God and His righteousness.

It's impossible for the majority of people to have life constructed so that they do things the same way every day. Many have made *order* the priority. If they do their devotionals every morning at 4:30, they are somehow holy. If they get to every one of their kids' games, they're better dads. But the Christian life is not about doing the same thing every day like a robot. It's about God being in control.

Our problem is that we tend to compartmentalize these three important relationships in our lives. We want to make specific times for each one, and if we don't do it the same each day, we begin to feel guilty and usually drop the thing that doesn't seem to be working out. Marriage and God are usually the first victims of our inability to do it right all the time.

Jesus didn't call us to differentiate ourselves by particular disciplines, but by solid relationships with Him and others, especially our wives. We need to know that there are times when work takes the priority, and other times when family takes the priority. But that can only happen when we're confident of who we are in Christ, have a strong and vital relationship with Christ, and know that God is in control. We also need to avoid abusing any of these three priorities.

COME TO ME AS LITTLE CHILDREN

Here is what we need to do: We need to become like children. My wife has a very bad knee, and one day she had so much pain that she almost fell in our driveway. My grandson Jimmy, who was 4, was walking with her. When I asked him to pray for Grams, he fell to the ground and began to pray for her knee. Later, at a theme park in Pittsburgh, I banged my knee against a table and it really hurt. Jimmy laid hands on my knee, then removed his hands and placed his head in them and quietly prayed for me. This was done with dozens of people sitting around us as we all ate lunch. When he was finished, Jimmy picked up his Slurpy and said, "How is it, Gramps?"

Since that time I've been watching Jimmy, and it is interesting to me that prayer is a normal part of his life at age 5. He can be eating, watching TV, walking with you, or drinking a Slurpy, and if you need prayer, he'll stop whatever he's doing and pray a simple prayer. When he's done praying, he picks up where he left off and goes on with what he was doing. Apparently, prayer was meant to be a normal part of life, like drinking a Slurpy.

No wonder Jesus said, "I tell you the truth, unless you change and become like little children, you will never enter the kingdom of heaven" (Matt. 18:3). I believe that to enter the kingdom of heaven, you need to enter the kingdom of God. Often these phrases are used interchangeably to mean the same thing. I believe God is telling us that if He is not in control, we cannot be a part of Him or His kingdom.

We're not talking about becoming childish. Rather, we are talking about becoming childlike and making sure we do the things that God has called us to in our lives. Childlike qualities are important for Christians to emulate. The childlike qualities of innocence, trust, humility, obedience, gentleness and seeking are perfectly appropriate for adults. In this case, our focus is seeking the kingdom of God in marriage and in the work that God has provided for us.

I'm convinced that if you desire God with all your heart, you will soon desire your wife with all your heart. When you desire your wife with all your heart, you will soon see your marriage develop according to God's plan and purpose—and your work will become more successful and enjoyable.

PUTTING IT ALL TOGETHER

One day I was thinking about the age-old questions Christians use to determine how godly you are. You may have been asked these questions at one time or another. The first question is, "What is the most important thing in your life?" If you don't say, "God," you are looked at strangely. The second question asks you to define the second most important thing in your life and that had better be "family" or once again you appear to fall short. The last answer people are looking for is, "work."

If you answer these wrong you can't be much of a Christian. But, if we knew the truth or spoke the truth we would soon recognize that the answers are actually reversed if we look at our passion and time spent with each. For most Christians the honest answers are, work, family and God, in that order.

Both family and God take a distant second and third place.

While I was thinking about this, God entered into my thoughts and said, "that's wrong." "Wrong," I said, "You are first aren't you?" He said, "Yes, I am. But what you have done is demean your wife and work by ranking them in a legalistic way." I asked God what He was saying and He placed a picture in my mind of three equal overlapping circles. You know the kind. There is a point where each circle shares the same spot. Its known as a VENN diagram.

God said, "I'm in that spot where all the circles overlap. Now, one circle is your relationship with me. Another circle is your relationship with your wife and the other circle is your relationship with your work. What I want you to see is that I am in all three of these areas of your life. Yes, you must spend time with me so we can become close, but there are going to be times when your wife needs your presence more then I do and you must go and spend the necessary time with her. Why? Because, I'm in your relationship with you and your wife as much as I am in your relationship with me. I want you to have a great marriage so people can see just how much I'm involved in marriages. I care about your marriage.

"Additionally, there are going to be seasons in your work life where you are not able to spend as much time with Me as you once did, but that's OK. You see I'm with you at work. I want you to succeed where I have called you so I can receive the glory of a godly man in the workplace.

What makes you think I appreciate the 15-30

minutes you give Me everyday only to leave Me in the closet and forget Me all day long until the next morning when you return to confess your sins and get fueled up for the next day? Once your morning quiet time is over, I never see you or hear from you again until the next day. Why would you leave Me in the closet? I want to be with you everywhere you go. I'm a 24/7/365 God.

"Now there is a caveat. You must never think that because I'm in all these relationships that you can ignore Me. You must always make time for Me, but on certain occasions your wife or work will need the best of you more then I do. Lighten up and follow Me wherever I go. Don't you think that if your wife is hurting that I won't be there? Most likely I will beat you there every time. Don't you want to be where I'm working? You'll simply meet Me there. The same is true of your work."

What God is looking for are obedient followers who know where God is going to show up and then join Him there. He hates legalism in whatever form it takes. This makes your life far more fluid and less stressful and far more in tune with where God is and where He wants you to be.

The fact of the matter is, we are to desire God, our wives and our work together. Each is supposed to be present in our heart, soul and mind at all times. When we desire God with all our hearts, our personal relationship with Him, our wives and our work become fluid instead of legalistic. This is why we can't compartmentalize God, marriage and work. God said that He will be with you always, and guess what? So are your wife and work. They are inseparable parts of your life.

We need to better understand what God has in store for us as a couple, and one of the most important and misunderstood areas is your wife's calling as the revealer of the enemy. The only way I can describe this is to make a direct comparison with physical DNA coding and what the results of that are.

PHYSICAL DNA CODING

We all know why our children and grandchildren look something like one of us or have other traits like us. There may even be a physical likeness to both parents. Some children look nothing like their parents but once you see an old picture of a distant relative you see a resemblance that is unmistakable. Genetic DNA coding goes on forever in a family line, and that is because God created us that way. There are even certain statistics that tell us that if a right-handed person marries a left-handed person, three of every four children will be right-handed. The same is true of eye color. The dominant genes are three times more likely to show up then the recessive genes. It's predictable.

SPIRITUAL DNA CODING

The term "revealer of the enemy" is one that is the Ancient Hebrew for helpmate. That's right. Your helpmate is considered, by God to be the revealer of the enemy. What does that mean? To see how this works itself out we have to visit Genesis 3:13 where, when asked by God, "What is this you have done?" Eve replies, "The serpent deceived me, and I ate." In other words, *We were face to face and while we were talking the serpent convinced me to do it. I saw his face.*

If she were that close there are two things she is saying here. First, I know his game now. He is a deceiver and a liar. You can't trust him. Second, Eve is saying I saw his face and I would recognize him anywhere. There is a movie called *Colateral Damage* that starred Arnold Schwarzenegger. In the movie his family car is blown up by a man, and his wife and children die. He is the only one who saw the man do it. While everyone wanted to help Arnold find the enemy, he was the only one who could recognize him. He saw his face and so it is with Eve and all women.

It is my impression that what we refer to as a woman's intuition and/or sixth sense is not that at all. What it really is, is God passing down the Spiritual DNA of Eve in recognizing the enemy and his schemes. Now, I can't make a scientific case for this as easily as physical DNA, and I'm not going to try to do so. I will simply say that we have never been able to understand why a woman is so protective of her siblings and yes, even her husband. Much of it is covered by what we refer to as "Mother's instinct."

My point in all of this as I relate it to my life and the lives of many I know is that what is often inexplicable is often God. I am convinced that God has passed this "revealer of the enemy" spiritual gene down to all women and it really starts paying off when a woman receives Christ as her Lord and Savior. I believe it is always there and is exhibited many times, but once we know why God gave this gift to women we can see how important it is for us to make sure it is activated to the fullest extent possible.

What activates it to the fullest extent possible is when the husband creates an environment conducive to holiness so his wife can operate in her spiritual gifts and become the spiritual covering of her husband's ministry at work. If the husband is doing his best to create holiness in the home, then his wife is going to be doing her best to reveal what the enemy is up to, and it becomes a beautiful circle that can go unbroken. When that happens the enemy is locked out of the marriage, home and ministry.

I hear men say "I never bring my job home." In other words, they never bring their job-related problems home to bother their wives. Why not? Their wives may be able to help them. Your wife is a part of all your life, and that includes any issues you have at work. Your helpmate is considered the "revealer" of the enemy. It is she who discerns and reveals to you the enemy's plans in your life and work. So, she needs to know what is happening at work.

Virtually every husband I have met at my seminars has told me that their wife has spoken into their lives many times but they didn't listen. One man in his 60's told me that as he looks back on this idea he has become convinced that every time he did not listen to his wife's advice, because she couldn't make a solid case for her reasoning, she was right on target.

Take your work home! Please!

FAVOR IS VERY GOOD

When you take your first step toward your destiny, God is there to guide you. He has already prepared in advance the works you are called to, and He is waiting for you to walk in them. And when you follow God's promises, He is not ashamed to be called your God. Tommy Tenney, in *The God Chasers*, writes, "God's favor flows wherever His face is directed." Tenney tells us that you can be God's child and not have His favor. So how do you get God's favor to flow in your direction? Humble yourself, pray and seek God's face.

I never knew or understood God's favor until A.J. and I heard God call us to Pittsburgh and agreed to follow without really knowing why. We didn't even know what the Lord was calling us to, but we sold our house and moved our businesses to Pittsburgh. We couldn't have done this unless we viewed God, marriage and work as joined together in God's plan for us.

Within a few months, doors began to open for me, and I began to meet with pastors and Christian leaders in the Pittsburgh area to advance the kingdom through prayer evangelism. How did that happen? Through the favor of God. I had no right to be received by these pastors, but I was. This type of favor has preceded me virtually everywhere I have gone in the past eight years.

The same favor and peace are available to you in your marriage, work, and ministry in the marketplace if God's desires become your desires. It's all about fulfilling your calling as a follower of Christ, a husband and a worker.

Your Spouse Is the Most Important Person in Your Life

Here's a thought for both men and women: your children are a gift from God, and you have a tremendous responsibility for them; but don't believe that they are the most important people in your life. Your spouse holds that place and always should. Your children will grow up and, most of the time, get married and move away. You may only see them once or twice a year. But your spouse is a different matter. He or she will be with you forever.

I once told my wife that she shouldn't ignore me while she was mothering the children; a time would come when they would leave, but I would still be around. I was kidding, but it's very true. The same thing can be said about our careers. When you are given a golden parachute at age 55 or retire at age 60 or 65, your wife will still be there. Will you know her? You will only know her if you've spent time with her prior to your retirement—only if you have desired her throughout all those years.

Perseverance is the key to a great move of God. We must begin with our marriages and persevere until they are holy. We must persevere in the marketplace until we see similar results. This will teach us how to persevere as the body of Christ, so we can see God manifest Himself throughout the whole world. Think about it: It needs to begin with you and millions who are like you, right there in the marketplace. But someone has to go first. You're only one step away. Can you take that step with me?

SUMMARY POINTS

- The difference between endurance and perseverance is the word *ability*.
- Endurance is the ability to finish a race, while perseverance is continuing to the end in spite of the difficulty and opposition you face.
- Desire is what drives us to persevere. Whatever you desire, you will go after wholeheartedly, in spite of pain, distress, fatigue, or hardship. Nothing will stop you.
- Our desires should be to have vital relationships with our Lord, our wife, our children and our work.

WHAT'S NEXT?

This book has been about a life-changing experience that needs to take place in virtually every Christian marriage if we are going to ever see a great move of God in the marketplace and in our cities. God is releasing marketplace people into ministry right where He has called them, so that cities can be reached for Christ. But your ministry in the marketplace will only advance to the extent that your marriage permits. Perhaps you're asking, "What do I do now?" Regardless of how long you've been married, God is God. He will be delighted to set you on the right path to bring about this necessary change.

It's often nothing more than a matter of focus. You started off wanting the best marriage ever, but somewhere along the way you lost your focus. You became single-minded about your career or something else of apparent importance, and your marriage became less important. Maybe you got bored with life in general, and everything lost its significance. Maybe you never thought your marriage was as important as your career. Most likely your focus on your marriage was vulnerable because it replaced what was to be the main focus: God. A divided focus causes you to be *generally* faithful. God requires us to be *fully* faithful to Him and Him alone. If you're faithful to God and obey Him in your marriage, all else will be perfect.

The Bible says, "The fear of the Lord is the beginning of wisdom" (Ps. 111:10). We need to seek our approval and esteem from God alone. Only He is constant and can satisfy our souls. Only He can give us the direction we need. Only He orders the steps of the righteous. What the world offers is temporary and quite mercurial in nature

The typical question after reading a book like this is, "How do I do what's next, now that I know I need to do something?" Many of us will say, "I just don't have enough faith." You're probably right, since "faith comes from hearing the message, and the message is heard through the word of Christ" (Rom. 10:17). But even faith as small as a mustard seed can move mountains. It's interesting to note that when Christ chose to give himself up for the church there was no church. He gave up his life through faith. We must do the same as a husband.

I am always asked, "What should I do next? This occurs when someone has read this book, heard the tape series or attended the seminar. It is very important to make sure that you begin at the beginning. That would be your marriage. The very first thing you need to do is sit down with your wife and discuss what you heard and what you think. We are encouraging everyone to get the book, tape series and study guides and work through these materials over a 10 week period.

I am convinced, and results have shown, that if you take the time to do this first you will begin to see how God will work everything out in your marriage and work. The mere fact that you choose to dig in will cause God to enlighten you about both aspects of your lives. Do this first and the rest of this chapter will make sense.

LIVE IT OUT DAY BY DAY AND STEP BY STEP

The first step is to let go of whatever form of human-determined success you are holding on to, so you can receive something of greater value from God. Work hard and smart, but don't expect your success in business to be what feeds your need for significance and approval. Seek your approval and significance from God, for only He is constant and can satisfy your soul.

The second step is to pray about your relationships with God, your wife and your work. Ask God to reveal what you need to do to see change come to pass.

The third step is to know that the Holy Spirit is the only one who can give you the ability to move forward in your marriage and career in a manner that is pleasing to God. Remember, the Bible tells us to be filled with the Holy Spirit (Eph. 5:18). Only He can give us the power to change.

The fourth step is to get into the Word of God. Check out the many verses I have used in this book as a starting point. Go back and study them, especially Philippians 2:1-4. God will use these Scriptures to lead you to other verses of equal importance.

The fifth step is to obey what you have read in the Word. "To obey is better than sacrifice" (1 Sam. 15:22). You don't have to understand why unconditional love is important in order to do it. Just do it because God said so. Starting with Philippians 2:1-4, you should begin to love your wife unconditionally, consider her better than yourself, consider her interests as equal to your own, and become one in purpose with your wife. Begin to make your home a place that is conducive to holiness so that your wife and children can see what holiness looks like. In other words, give yourself up for your wife as Christ gave Himself up for the church (Eph. 5:25-27). This won't happen all at once; it's a process.

The sixth step is to recognize the importance of the three major components in your life: your relationship with God, your wife, and your work. Know that God is always at the center of your life, but that your ministry in the workplace will only advance to the extent that your marriage permits. These two, marriage and work, are dependent upon each other and are both dependent on God. You will only be fully successful in your work if you have the proper order God requires in your life.

The seventh step is to determine who, within the marketplace, is in your sphere of influence, and with whom, among the Christians in your workplace, God would have you pray. It's better to start with one or two others to build the unity and staying power it will take to reach your sector of the marketplace for Christ. True unity is about being cohesive, not inclusive. Just as you are becoming like-minded in your marriage, you must become united in the marketplace. It is very difficult to be cohesive with a bunch of people you have never had a relationship with in the past. That's why it's important to let God direct you to one or two people; after that, let God give the increase as well.

Along with praying with a few other Christians, it is important that you begin to pray for those with whom you come in contact on a regular basis— people like your boss, your secretary, your customers, and other employees.

Luke 10 provides a model you can use comfortably throughout your marketplace ministry. You will note that when Jesus sent out the 70, He told them that the harvest was plentiful, but that the workers were few. There was nothing wrong with the harvest or the workers. The problem was that the workers were not working the harvest field.

Here is what Jesus told the 70 to do, and it applies to us today in the marketplace.

A. *Pray peace upon their houses.* Simply put, begin to bless and pray for those you know at work. Don't tell them. Just pray for them. Blessings are powerful and will begin to change the spiritual climate in your work-place. This may go on for months, until you are told to...

B. *Eat what they put before you.* This simply

means to fellowship with your associates. In other words, go to lunch or go shopping with them. Maybe you can have them over to your house. Get to know the lost and develop relationships with them. Become a friend of sinners. Jesus did. After developing a relationship with them, you are able to...

C. *Heal the sick*. This means we are to pray for the felt needs of the lost. Every person has needs that only God can answer, and this is true of the lost. After you have fellowshipped with them, you may want to tell them, in a casual moment, that you have been praying for them in a very general way that God would bless them. Ask them if they have any needs that only God could answer. When they tell you, tell them you will be praying for them and that they should keep you informed of what is happening. When God answers your prayers for them, you can then...

D. Tell them that the kingdom of God is near them. After God answers their prayers, they will want to thank you or find out how it all happened. Simply tell them that God came near them because He loves them and wants to have a relationship with them. Now, you can give testimony to who God is in your life.

The eighth step is the stage at which you must be on your own. No other situation will be quite like yours—in marriage or in the marketplace.

Once you find one or two people to pray with in the marketplace and are becoming the spiritual head of your home, God will begin to speak to you about the road you are going to take. It will be a truly unique one.

You stand at the threshold of a great move of God in your life, your marriage, your marketplace and your city. From my own experience, I believe that this is the best trip you can ever take. And when it is completed, you'll hear the words every Christian longs to hear: "Well done, good and

HOW TO SPREAD THE WORD; A NEW STRATEGY

While at a Harvest Evangelism conference in Argentina my book was read by three women who had purchased it prior to the conference. When they arrived at the conference they began to casually talk about the book at various meals and soon the attendees were asking me where they could get the book. Due to the discussion raised by these three women we sold every book we brought and they are now in the hands of people who live in Hong Kong, Philippines, South Africa, Canada and other countries.

On the last day of the conference I had lunch with two businessmen who have been friends of Harvest for a number of years. Larry Ihle lives in Minneapolis and Dick Hochreiter in Southern California. As we entered into the lobby of the hotel they stopped me and Dick said, "Jack, your message is so important to the body of Christ that you are going to sell 500,000 copies of the book."

Needless to say I was totally dumbfounded since it is self-published and those numbers are unheard of in that arena. Then Larry said, "No, No Dick. Jack is going to sell a minimum of one million books and he will sell them by December 31, 2005."

I said, "This is great guys but how do you think that will happen?" Larry set us praying right in the middle of the Hilton Hotel lobby and when we were finished he said, "Send me 100 books and Dick you need a 100 too, don't you?" Dick said, "That's the number God put on my heart as you were praying." Later they determined they needed a case, which are 100 books. Larry then said, "Here is what God has shown me as to how it is going to happen. Dick and I are going to be giving these books out as gifts to friends, colleagues, church members and anyone God shows us. We'll ask them to read the book and let us know what they think. Those who come back with a favorable report will be asked to do what we did, buy a case of books and give them away. As the book is given away over the next three years we will see God spread it across the world. As a matter of fact Dick and I will talk with all the people who attended the conference and ask them to join us."

You need to know that on our way to the airport to return home a woman from the conference asked me about the book and bought a case to do what Larry and Dick are doing. Then another man from the conference bought a case a week later. Then two cases were sold in Tampa at a seminar and one man is determining whether he wants one, two or three cases. Larry and Dick hadn't even spoken to the attendees yet and in two weeks we sold 7 cases, which is almost as many as we sold in the first nine months. There seems to be a fresh release on the book since that prayer in the lobby. As of this writing we have sold 18 cases. That's why this reprinting of 10,000 copies is taking place.

If God has touched you through this book, and you have the ability to buy a case would you consider joining the group of marketplace people who are giving this book as a gift to spread the message worldwide? The cost per case is $1,000 for 100 books. You can pay it in full or spread it over 12 months. There are those who can't afford a case of books but would like to buy ten, twenty or more. If that's you please let us know. The books are $10 each.

I'm attaching the letter that Larry and Dick have sent out to the conference attendees so you can see what they are saying. Please use this as you see fit. May you be blessed with a Godly marriage as you move forward in reaching your sphere of influence for Christ.

Dear Friend,

Dick Hochreiter and I were talking with Jack Serra one afternoon and God showed Dick and I that Jacks book, Marketplace, Marriage and Revival was going to sell at least one million copies by December 31, 2005. Dick and I truly believe that the message in Jacks book must be released to as many believers as possible and God has given us a plan to accomplish that.

God has shown us that we need to market Jacks book in a unique way. What we see happening is very simple and does not require a large financial investment on anyone's part. We are looking for at least 100 marketplace people to purchase a case of Jacks book and give them away to the Christians in their sphere of influence. There are 100 books in a box and the cost would be $1,000 per box.

As we distribute the books we simply ask each person to read it and let us know what they think. When they return with a positive response we ask them to do what we are doing, buy a box and pass the book on to 100 others. They would also ask their people to invest in the book as well. This would go forward until God stops it.

To show you how simple this is and how fast it can happen, we know that if only 30 people buy a box initially and they hand the books out to 100 people and they only have 10 people buy a case of the books and these people repeat the process we can see one million books given away in just four stages. Actually, if that occurred we would have sold 30,000 cases and that would be 3 million books given away.

The actual number required to give away one million books with 30 original investors is something like 4.5 people out of each 100 who receive the book for four stages.

THE OBJECTIVES OF THIS PLAN ARE AS FOLLOWS:

1) Get the book and message in the hands of Christians who need to hear it so we can see marriages transformed and marketplace Christians effective in their calling. Your sphere of influence could be people you know at work or church. Other areas are neighbors, friends and family. Obviously, the primary candidate is a Christian marketplace person.

2) Give those who purchase the book an opportunity to see their financial investment in action and directly impacting lives of people they know.

3) Determine to have about 10-12 who receive the book do what you have done in their sphere of influence. Have them buy a box of books and give them away with the same challenge.

4) Support the ministry so the Kingdom of God can be built in marriages, the marketplace and the city.

You need to know that the money from selling the books ends up in a Harvest Evangelism, Inc. special account to build the Kingdom of God. Jack and A.J. are the Trustees of the account. Over eighty percent of all profits will go to building the Kingdom of God. Thirty-six percent of all profits will go to Harvest to build the Kingdom of God and thirty-six percent will go to help the poor.

Please let us know if you are able to join us in this great adventure.

Blessings,

Larry Ihle and Dick Hochreiter

You can contact Jack and AJ directly by email, mail or calling them.

Jack and AJ Serra, Sr
PO Box 656
Murrysville, PA 15668

harvestmmr@aol.com

412-400-0135

MARKETPLACE, MARRIAGE & REVIVAL
TAPE SERIES

Six messages based on Jack's seminar. The messages are organized into six 30-45 minute teachings from the book that are full of practical applications that compliment the book. Price $20.

MARKETPLACE, MARRIAGE & REVIVAL
STUDY GUIDE

A companion guide to be used with the book and tape series. The study guide is for couples, small groups, Sunday School groups, men's groups and other small groups. There is some additional information included in this guide. The study includes 10 lessons. Price $4 each and two for $6.

MARKETPLACE, MARRIAGE & REVIVAL
STUDY PACKAGE

One book, one tape series and two study guides. Each couple needs their own package so they can read the book and listen to the assigned tapes prior to the meeting. 10 lessons are included. Price $30.

COMING IN 2004

GRANDPARENTS, GRANDCHILDREN AND REVIVAL; THE SPIRITUAL CONNECTION

As a parent, grandparent and student of revival, Jack Serra, SR has written a book for grandparents so they can better understand the tremendous calling on their lives. So often we see grandparents feeling as though they have little or no significance to their lives. One of the most important ministries a grandparent can have is found right in his own family. God tells us we are to train up our children and their children after them. If we are going to see a great move of God we must pass our spiritual experience down the generational lines.

For more information about the ministry, to purchase materials or to learn about Jack's seminars,

Contact: Jack Serra, SR
Email: harvestmmr@aol.com
Mail: Harvest Evangelism Eastern Region,
           PO Box 656, Murrysville, PA 15668
Phone: 412-400-0135

"DO OVERS" COUNT

CHAPTER TWO

GRANDPARENTS DO GET A SECOND CHANCE

"Your faithfulness continues through all generations." Psalm 119:90

THE ULTIMATE "DO OVER"

Do you remember when you were a kid; try hard now grandparents, and you were able to call out, "DO OVER", when you were playing? If you made a mistake at something and wanted to do it again you could just yell out, "DO OVER"? It wasn't like cheating because everyone did it and it was fair for everyone to say it. It was just something that was understood. It's kind of like a mulligan in golf. A mulligan is often allowed on the first tee when you're just out playing the game for fun. You're certainly not in a tournament. If you hit a ball on the first tee and you don't like it you can hit another ball and play it without any penalty. That's a mulligan and it is definitely a "DO OVER."

Oh, how many times in life would it have been helpful to be able to just call out, "DO OVER." Maybe you wanted to cry out, "Do Over", during a baseball game when you struck out with the bases loaded in the last inning or how about the job you took and wished you hadn't a few months later. It might have been when you got that ticket for speeding or when you said something awful to a friend or your spouse. How about the time you failed an important test because you didn't study hard enough? A definite "DO OVER". Some of you may have lost quite a few years during your teens and would love to have them back "DO OVER"!!! "DO OVER"!!!

I can imagine that you're thinking about a number of times you would have liked to yell out, "DO OVER" at the top of your voice. When you yelled at your son or daughter and felt so terrible about it would have been a perfect time for a "DO OVER", wouldn't it? How about when you told a lie and you wanted to pull the words back into your mouth, but couldn't? It was too late. What a time for a "DO OVER."

There are many times when I promised God I wouldn't commit that sin again, but I did. Oh, how I wanted to have a "DO OVER" for that time. By the way, God is the only one who can truly grant a "DO OVER", if you ask for him to forgive you. You basically start all over again with a clean slate. Now that is the ultimate "DO OVER", but it was very costly for God to give us another chance and we certainly don't want to abuse his grace and mercy by continually calling out, "DO OVER."

WOULD YOU LIKE TO RAISE YOUR KIDS AGAIN?

If you're married or have been married and your children are grown, I'm sure there has been a time or two when you wished that you could have one more opportunity to raise your children again. Things would certainly be different, wouldn't they? You know that you would never give in the way you did the first time. You would have been there for them more than you were. You probably wouldn't have missed a ball game, dance review or piano recital. You would have taken more time just to talk with them and play with them. How many times did you say no to their simple requests? Not this time. It would definitely be different this time. Yes, would be the order of the day when they asked you to read to them, go to the park, help fly their new kite or just play catch before dinner.

The list goes on and on. Most lists are pretty much the same, while having some slight variations. Cat Stevens sang a song about this issue. The son kept asking his dad to play and the dad kept telling him later. Unfortunately, later never came and the son didn't have time for his dad when his dad had time for him.

In the movie, "I Am Sam", the question asked of the father, Sam, who was the mental equivalent of a six year old was, "What does it take to be a good father." His answer was quite good. Sam said, "Constancy; Patience; Listening, even when you don't want to, and Love." Not bad for a father with a six year olds mental capacity.

You Become What You Learn

Children often become what they learn from their parents. They learn how to say no and they learn that other things are more important then a dad playing with the kids. After all they learned from you, didn't they?

I have some very good news for you if you're a grandparent. There is a partial "DO OVER" regarding children. They're called grandchildren. That's right, you get another chance when God gives you grandchildren. I know it's not a real "DO OVER", but it is as important as your first shot at kids. We can't ever get back the times we've lost and we can't alter what we did wrong by reliving the time so we can finally do it right. From the standpoint of time those times and days are lost forever. Today is today and we have to live in the present and learn from our past and do things right this time.

The only thing we can do if we believe we have in some way wronged our children is to ask their forgiveness. That is the great thing about being a Christian. We can be forgiven by God and man, if we simply ask. If you truly believe you have sinned in some way towards your child or children then go to them and tell then how you feel and apologize and ask them for their forgiveness. I did that with two of my children. One didn't even remember the incident, but I did and I knew I was wrong.

Maybe something has come to mind as you have been reading this. If so, pray about it and do something about it. If you have sinned regarding your children you need to confess that so you can go before your children's children with a clean slate. If you don't your efforts to touch your grand-children could be limited.

THE SPIRITUAL "DO OVER"

You may have noticed that I left out a very important part of the "DO OVER" for most of us. This is where, I believe, you get your most important "DO OVER". If we had the opportunity to do it all over again with our children many of us would need to do a far better job regarding the spiritual side of life. At least AJ and I could have done a lot better. There are so many things we could have done differently so that our children could have known Christ or known Him earlier in life.

If your children don't know Christ you must continue to love them unconditionally and live a holy life while doing so. It's never too late for God to touch your children. Don't give up on them.

Now, however, you have a fresh start with your grandchildren. Will they see the same person their parent did or will they see someone who is ready to begin their "DO OVER"? and do it right this time? Join me in looking at the ULTIMATE "DO OVER"!

To order: Grandparents, Grandchildren and
             Revival: The Spiritual Connection,
             Call: 412-400-0135